THE
Mystery Tradition
OF
Miraculous Conception

MARY AND THE LINEAGE OF VIRGIN BIRTHS

Marguerite Mary Rigoglioso, Ph.D.

Bear & Company
Rochester, Vermont

Bear & Company
One Park Street
Rochester, Vermont 05767
www.BearandCompanyBooks.com

Text stock is SFI certified

Bear & Company is a division of Inner Traditions International.

Cataloging-in-Publication Data for this title is available from the Library of Congress.

ISBN 978-1-59143-413-9 (print)
ISBN 978-1-59143-414-6 (ebook)

Printed and bound in the United States by Lake Book Manufacturing, Inc.
The text stock is SFI certified. The Sustainable Forestry Initiative® program promotes sustainable forest management.

10 9 8 7 6 5 4 3 2 1

Text design and layout by Virginia Scott Bowman
This book was typeset in Garamond Premier Pro with Mackay and Trenda used as the display typefaces.

To send correspondence to the author of this book, mail a first-class letter to the author c/o Inner Traditions • Bear & Company, One Park Street, Rochester, VT 05767, and we will forward the communication, or contact the author directly at **www.sevensistersmysteryschool.com**.

＊

To Mother Mary, Star of the Infinite Sea

Contents

✳

Appendix
Birth of Mary (Infancy Gospel of James)

Acknowledgments

I offer my gratitude to the many beautiful souls who have responded with such enthusiasm to my online courses through Seven Sisters Mystery School, particularly Mary, Conscious Priestess of Divine Birth, which was the seed for this book, and the Mother Mary Mystery Teachings: Your Pathway to Love, Healing, and Inner Divinity. Thanks also to those who have been supporters from the beginning through your participation in my Divine Birth Mystery Teachings and related workshops and lectures, as well as to the women in my Priestess of the Dove Oracle Trainings. Your validation and reflections have given me encouragement and have helped me amplify and deepen my work.

I also thank the following people who have provided further inspiration, validation, or support for my work on Mary: "Laurie," Maura McCarley Torkildson, Charlene Spretnak, Lucia Chiavola Birnbaum, Mary Beth Moser, Robert Owings, Maureen Walton, Karen Holmes, Cindy Lindsay, Swami Sri Kaleshwar, Den Poitras, Christy Michaels, Diana Melchizedek, Angela de la Agua, Colette De Gagnier-Rettner, Carmen Nash, Bob Crimi, Ava Park, Graell Corsini, Vajra Ma, Amejo Amyot, Connie Viveros, Andrée Morgana, Joy Reichard, Elizabeth Barton, Shannon Werner, Catherine Ann Clemett, Claire Heartsong, Patricia Anderson, Byron Belitsos, and Bill Gladstone. I thank Jeremy Hultin as well, for his generous and cheerful assistance with some of the ancient Greek.

And of course, my gratitude goes out to the one known as Isis/Mary/Sophia/Mother Divine, for the teachings on the path.

CHAPTER 1

Let It Be Revealed

The Hour of a New Mary

The Virgin Mary's time has come. In fact, we are long overdue for a revolutionary understanding of her that frees her from dogmatic baggage and restores her to her rightful place as a great holy woman. In recent decades, thousands of readers worldwide of books such as Meggan Watterson's *Mary Magdalene Revealed,* Cynthia Borgeault's *The Meaning of Mary Magdalene,* and Margaret Starbird's *The Woman with the Alabaster Jar* have awoken to another Mary, Mary Magdalene, who is not a prostitute, but rather a consort of Jesus. Now is the moment for us to recognize the Divine Feminine figure of *Mother* Mary, not as a passive bystander to her own pregnancy, but rather as a specialized priestess who deliberately planned and carried out the miraculous conception of her son.

To uncover a Magdalene who was a powerful sacred woman, nothing less than the chief of the apostles, we have had to look to suppressed gospels about her, some of which have only reemerged from the sands of time in the twentieth century. The remarkable discoveries about her have been a thrilling development for many around the planet who are seeking role models of female empowerment and who may have intuited that there was far more to the Magdalene than what the New Testament says about her.

As with Magdalene, the day of dawning has now come for Mother Mary. Who was this most famous of women, really, and what was her conception of Jesus all about? We hear painfully little about her from the canonical gospels of Matthew, Mark, Luke, and John. Where we find a mother lode of information about her and her miraculous event is far outside of those books, in a little-known writing called the Infancy Gospel of James (also known as the Protevangelium of James), which became the basis of Mary's feast days in the church calendar. It is on this gospel that I throw the floodlights in this book to reveal the truth about Mary, a truth that is ancient but will seem new to many readers. The truth is that Mary indeed did conceive Jesus in a miraculous way. But she did so not through some kind of divine force that was using her body for its own agenda; she accomplished this feat through a careful process that she willed and initiated, and for which she was trained by a lineage of holy women before her.

In my two previous books I uncovered extensive evidence that this form of miraculous conception did occur in the ancient world. Now, in this book, I boldly show that Mary was born into a family and a history of women who possessed, cultivated, and passed on the ability to consciously conceive elevated beings to help the planet. These were specialized women schooled in what I call the "womb mysteries," secret knowledge of the capabilities of the human womb, including divine birth, which women all over the ancient world shared with other promising candidates over thousands of years. Mary was one of several powerful priestesses in her family and ancestry who had command over the human conception process, and she took this art to a whole new level.

All of this is precisely what her infancy gospel tells us—if you know how to look. No one has known how to look before now, however, because they have lacked the broader historical view of divine birth as an actual practice of real women that spanned the ancient Mediterranean world and beyond. In my hours, days, months, and years of scholarly sifting and sorting through ancient records, culminating in my two previous books, *The Cult of Divine Birth in Ancient Greece* and *Virgin Mother Goddesses of Antiquity*, I pieced together that history. And as a result I have been able to bring this knowledge to bear in decoding what Mary's gospel has been hiding in plain sight for nearly two thousand years. That deciphering is what this book is about.

In *The Mystery Tradition of Miraculous Conception* you will discover not only how Mary consciously conceived Jesus in an extraordinary way, but also how she herself was divinely conceived by her mother, Anne. That means you will come to recognize that Mary herself was born as an embodiment of something much needed in the ancient world and even more so in today's world: the Divine Feminine, in all of her power and wisdom. Knowing the base of potency from which she operated will help you see why Mary was able to bring forth an especially high-level embodiment of the Divine from her own body for the benefit of humanity. You will glimpse into how she was trained, when, and by whom, as well as some of the esoteric techniques she used to fulfill her ministry in this regard.

This book also uncovers the fact that Mary and Anne's lineage of divine-birth priestesses went all the way back to Sarah, the wife of the biblical patriarch Abraham and the great matriarch of Hebrew culture. We will see how this lineage extended across their family to include Elizabeth, who was not only the mother of the miraculously born John the Baptist, but who also may have been Anne's sister.

By exploring the reality of Mary as a trained agent in divine conception, this book corrects the impression the New Testament has given us of a passive and bewildered girl, an incidental receptacle who had no idea what was happening to her beyond a short pronouncement by the Angel Gabriel. It also corrects the view that her virginity was a sign of her moral purity and that strict chastity is therefore something to be imposed on all women.

The Mystery Tradition of Miraculous Conception puts this sacred woman in her rightful place, front and center in the story of Jesus, as the pivot point around which the entire Christed enterprise unfolded. By showing that Mary was a conscious actor who deliberately intended for Jesus to come into our world, as well as a priestess whose celibacy was a chosen practice needed for this task, this book restores her as the empowered feminine orchestrator of these significant events.

What's more, by showing how, when, where, and why virgin birth could have been accomplished, this book also allows thinking people to make sense of Mary's miraculous conception of Jesus at long last. Prior to this, people have either had to accept the notion on blind faith, politely skirt around it as an embarrassing artifact, or dismiss it altogether as a bizarre claim. Now they have a clear and cogent alternative way of looking at this remarkable phenomenon that allows them to embrace the idea with intelligence. This book is intended to be the start of an inspired movement to restore Mary as the greatest holy woman who ever walked the Earth. With this book we are taking an important first step toward getting that fuller understanding of Mary by focusing especially on her powers of conception. In doing so we are further anchoring true feminine spiritual power more broadly. By showing what was possible for Mary and her female kin, we are setting the stage for women to understand the powers that lie within their own wombs, for Mary's abilities were not hers alone, but were—and are—capabilities open to all women who wish to go deeper on their spiritual path.

The Mystery Tradition of Miraculous Conception offers you a profound journey into the mystery of Mother Mary that no one has yet taken in all of the centuries that have passed since this most holy of women lived, and in all of the books that have been written about her. It invites *you*, as a reader, to reflect on and respond to what you are reading on the Seven Sisters Mystery School Facebook page. This book is the beginning of a "Mary-olution," one inviting the conscious participation of the broader global community.

Let it begin!

CHAPTER 2

Revealing the Hidden
Mystery of Divine Birth

To help you understand Mary as a conscious priestess of divine conception, let me take you on a brief foray into divine birth as uncovered in my two previous books, *The Cult of Divine Birth in Ancient Greece* and *Virgin Mother Goddesses of Antiquity*. This is critical background that has been missing in deciphering Mary's story. Having it available here will make it easier for you to make sense of the revelations about Mary in the coming chapters. It will give you a sense of some of the technologies she used and will reveal that Mary was part of a worldwide tradition that is only now being unveiled. Later in this book we will explore specific evidence from the gospel about her early life—that Mary indeed belonged to such a priestesshood, and that she was probably the most skilled priestess of her kind ever to have lived.

For now, let's look at evidence for parthenogenesis, the scientific word for what we might otherwise call *miraculous conception* or *virgin birth,* but I will distinguish biological parthenogenesis from what I'm identifying in this context as an advanced shamanic art exclusive to women. You'll hear about long-standing beliefs in women's ability to have sex with spirits, and you'll learn about the stages that the practice of virgin birth, also known as *divine birth,* went through over time as it degenerated. You'll come to understand the role of virginity, plant medicine, and trance states in this spiritual art, as well as how erotic energy also figured into it. Finally, you'll see how the practice was transmitted through lineages, how it was related to star lore and various important symbols, and how it may have involved the incorporation of a special diet.

THE GREATEST WOMEN'S SHAMANIC PRACTICE

To understand how divine birth is something Mary and her kin could have consciously practiced, it is helpful to first look at the fascinating concept known as *siddhi*. Siddhi is a Sanskrit word that has come to mean a supernatural or magical ability that is developed through spiritual activities such as meditation, chanting mantras, working with sacred drawings and symbols, and other forms of advanced spiritual practice. Hindu and Buddhist texts refer to such siddhis as the ability to walk through walls, read other people's minds, change the metabolism of your body, live on air, not cast a shadow, and even . . . walk on water. Yes, there are people documented as having been able to do all these things, and more.*

Now let's think about it: What about being able to conceive a child through one's body without sperm? For a woman, would this not be the ultimate siddhi? I say yes. Yet self-conception is generally not included in the siddhis we find listed in traditional sources. I contend this is because most of the spiritual texts that have come down to us focus on men and male achievements.

Yet we actually *do* see this kind of womanly achievement described—not in writings about siddhis, though. Instead, we see it in the miraculous birth stories that form nothing less than the foundations of numerous religions and entire cultures. In Judaism, for example, we have Sarah, who miraculously conceived Isaac in her elder years. In the Buddhist tradition, Maya is said to have given birth to Siddhartha Gautama, who became the Buddha, through unusual means. In Taoism we are told that the virgin Lao conceived Lao-Tzu by the sight of a falling star. In Zoroastrianism, legend says that the mother of Zarathustra

---

*See, for example, Yoga Sutras of Patanjali IV.1 for mention of how siddhic powers may arise and Subramuniyaswami, 817, for a discussion of siddhis.

(aka Zoroaster) conceived him by drinking a cup of haoma or soma, the sacred drink that so often figures in Persian and ancient Hindu legends. Indigenous North Americans also have traditions in which virgins give birth to beings who quickly develop the characteristics of miracle workers. For the Tsalagi (Cherokee), one such miraculously born (and reincarnating) spirit teacher is known as the Pale One, Wotan. The Haudenosaunee (Iroquois) talk about the divinely conceived Peacemaker.

So we do have records of the siddhic practice of miraculous birth, but these are often presented as events that must be accepted on blind faith. The stories never talk about the women involved being spiritual adepts who worked hard to be able to accomplish divine pregnancies. Instead, they present these female figures in passing, as passive vehicles to the experience. Because these accounts don't go any further and deeper into women's realities, they usually end up being written off as fictions.

I offer a different story. I have done deep excavation on this topic, looking specifically at the case of ancient Greece. Through careful research I have found in the ancient records from that place and time plentiful evidence that special priestesses dedicated to divine birth attempted to conceive children in various unusual ways as a real living practice. What I have uncovered is that the purpose of this practice was to bring very special beings to the planet. This research, of course, naturally led me to a deeper understanding of what Mary is all about.

I have come to understand that divinely born children were always seen as avatars; that is, incarnations of divinities. These divinely born ones are described in ancient religious stories and legends as being heroes or heroines, gifted spiritual leaders, demigods, or full-fledged deities. In fact, it was believed that such advanced beings could *only* incarnate through nonordinary methods of conception; it is the power they were endowed with by virtue of being born in these ways that allowed them to serve and elevate humanity in extraordinary ways.

As I pieced together this puzzle, I began to see that for a priestess, divinely conceiving a child was considered to be the highest level of spiritual achievement possible. It was regarded as graduating from the human level to the divine, particularly if she agreed to go through a certain kind of ritual death to seal the experience. As a result, such a woman usually became publicly honored in some way. Sometimes she was called a nymph or a heroine. Sometimes she had towns, hills, lakes, or oceans named after her. Sometimes she was worshipped as a full-fledged deity herself. This, as we shall see, is what happened with Mary.

Such priestesses' divinely born children also typically became the focus of worship, particularly after they left their human bodies. This was especially the case if they agreed to undergo a ritual sacrificial murder. We see this with Jesus, but hints of it are also present in other stories in the ancient world. Asclepius, for example, who was divinely conceived by a priestess named Coronis, rose to the level of divinity after dying by thunderbolt (that is, lightning). Being struck by lightning, I have come to understand, is something holy men of antiquity sometimes sought out because it provided a very great spiritual initiation, whether they lived or died as a result of the experience. And sure enough, Asclepius transformed from a human into the god of healing. Operating on the inner planes from that point onward, he was widely consulted in his special temples by those in the Greco-Roman world seeking remedies for their physical and emotional ailments. And people were indeed healed, on both the emotional and the physical levels.

We also have the story of Heracles, the son of Alcmene (by the god Zeus), who was poisoned by his wife. His strange choice to get himself to the top of a funeral pyre as he was dying is explained when we understand that he needed to have a proper ritual death, not an ignominious murder, in order to fully become divine. In other words, he had to beat the poison to the punch and die through a proper ritual if he was going to rise to godhood. He succeeded, which is why we remember him now as a supernatural being.

What I have found is that divine-birth priestesses could be found across the entire Mediterranean world, including North Africa and the Middle East, and beyond, spanning the world.* However, for the most

---

*For a more comprehensive survey of divine birth across the world, see Den Poitras, *Parthenogenesis: Women's Long-Lost Ability to Self-Conceive.*

part that information has been covered over for millennia as religious information has been filtered through a patriarchal perspective, first by the ancient writers themselves, and then by Western scholars.

IS DIVINE CONCEPTION REALLY POSSIBLE?

Divine birth in most cases was thought to involve some kind of parthenogenesis, which comes from the Greek *parthénos,* "virgin" or "maiden," and *gígnesthai,* "to be born." In other words, parthenogenesis means the conception and birth of a child in which male sperm is not involved.

In the scientific world we hear of various types of animals that are able to conceive parthenogenetically, particularly when they are under environmental stress or conditions of isolation. I wrote all about this in *The Cult of Divine Birth in Ancient Greece,* and since then I have occasionally seen news articles pop up about the latest female lizard, snake, shark, or other animal that under captivity or unusual circumstances has had a virgin birth. Because people know I have written about this topic, they like to send such articles my way. In the case of sea urchins and other creatures, scientists have also experimented with coaxing female eggs to divide. How? By using either electric shock or chemicals. One fertility researcher I have spoken with named Jerry L. Hall said he succeeded in having mice eggs start dividing when he exposed them to a special chemical.* He then put the zygotes back in the mice mothers' wombs, where they proceeded to grow. Hall personally told me that at that point the National Institutes of Health shut down the experiment, supposedly due to the fact that the experiment breached medical ethics.

Or was the possibility of parthenogenesis just too threatening to the patriarchal medical establishment?

So . . . parthenogenesis *is* biologically possible. But keep in mind that all of these situations in nature and laboratories concern parthenogenesis on a purely biological level. With divine birth we are talking about a spiritual practice. This would have been a high-level shamanic

---

*This was from a phone call with Jerry L. Hall on August 17, 2004. For more on this see Kolata's "Scientist Clones Human Embryos, and Creates an Ethical Challenge."

art for women, something very difficult to accomplish. This is why it was reserved mainly for the holy orders, understood to be an uncommon occurrence, and largely kept hidden as a mystery practice.

As is often the case in my research, after coming to my own intuitive conclusions about such things, I frequently find evidence in ancient writings to support my ideas. This happened most dramatically after I developed the historical time line for divine birth that I will share with you shortly. In my continued reading, I synchronistically located an ancient passage in one of the Nag Hammadi texts directly confirming the fact that people once believed women could indeed parthenogentically give birth to children in a sacred way. This text, dated to the first or second century of the Common Era (CE, previously called AD), discusses the conception of a male figure known as Seth, whom some have equated with Jesus. Here is the intriguing relevant passage, from the Revelation [or Apocalypse] of Adam, which I will explore with you in what follows: "[F]rom the nine Muses one separated. She came to a high mountain and spent some time seated there so that she desired her own body in order to become androgynous. She fulfilled her desire and became pregnant from her desire. He [the illuminator] was born."

The reference to the woman being a Muse, one of those female beings who grants supernatural knowledge to humans, suggests that what's being described is actually a priestess of the oracular tradition. In other words, the text is identifying her as an ancient prophetess. Moreover, I believe that what's being revealed in this passage is the process of a sacred woman "sitting on a mountain"; in other words, going into a state of deep meditation, a nonordinary or open state of consciousness. In this state she engages in what might be called a profound tantric erotic encounter with herself in order to spontaneously conceive. In short, this holy woman is doing high-level sex magic, and it's important to note for what is to come in our discussion of Mary that according to this description, such magic does involve desire; that is, sexual feelings and erotic energy. What's more, it results in the birth of an avatar.

Let me take a moment to emphasize that we are not talking about a practice that was (or is) intended to do away with men or make them unneeded. Rather, parthenogenesis, or divine birth, was—and potentially still is—a specialized activity with a very elevated purpose, available only to women of great spiritual advancement.

SEX WITH SPIRITS

The exploration of divine birth quickly brings us to the topic of women's ability to engage sexually with nonhuman beings.

What? Sex with gods? Yes.

As just one ancient case of this, we can look to Egypt. According to the ancient Greek writer Plutarch, the Egyptians believed it was indeed possible for a divine spirit to have sexual intercourse with a woman and make her pregnant "so as to breed in her the first beginnings of a generation."[1] This ancient declaration reveals an unusual conception process different from but related to parthenogenesis—namely, one in which a human woman can be impregnated by a disembodied spirit. According to this ancient belief, she then becomes the founder of an entire lineage of special human beings.

This may ring a bell for you if you know anything about ancient Egypt. We hear of such sacred unions between human queens and Egyptian male gods in various Egyptian texts, temple inscriptions, and imagery, particularly from the New Kingdom period (around 1550–1070 BCE). This type of union is famously said to have resulted in the birth of the pharaohs.[2] After developing my theories on divine birth based on mountains of information I collected by scouring ancient Greek writings, I once again found a remarkable confirmation of the ancient belief that a woman could have sexual relations with a being on the astral or unseen planes. This was in another text taken from one of the sections of the Testaments of the Twelve Patriarchs, twelve connected documents that purport to record the last words and exhortations of the twelve sons of Jacob, dated to the second or third century CE. Not only does this passage affirm that a woman could have sex with a spirit, it also specifically points to the belief that she could become pregnant from that interaction. This is dense, so give it a read, and I will then lead you through it:

[Human women] charmed the Watchers, who were before the Flood. As they continued looking at the women, they were filled with desire for them and perpetrated the act in their minds. Then they were transformed into human males, and while the women were cohabitating with their husbands they appeared to them. Since the women's minds were filled with lust for these apparitions, they gave birth to giants. For the Watchers were disclosed to them as being as high as the heavens.[3]

What are we talking about here? First, regarding the cast of characters, what we have in this passage are the "Watchers," divine messenger-beings that I understand are described in several postbiblical texts. These texts indeed affirm that the children of such beings were born of human women, that they were gigantic, and that they were known as the Nephilim.[4]

Surprisingly, this story also appears much earlier, in Genesis 6:1–4, where the interdimensional beings who impregnate human women are referred to as "sons of God." The text implies that the Nephilim are the children born of the interdimensional intercourse these sons of God engage in with the human women. Here in this biblical reference, another detail is added: the Nephilim are described as "the heroes that were of old, warriors of renown."* This characterization affirms the conclusion I came to in looking at the Greek material, that the children conceived by women by means of sex with gods (or, earlier, parthenogenesis) were considered special or elevated in some way.

The Testament of Reuben passage also gives us an intriguing glimpse of the process by which interdimensional impregnation can happen. It tells us that these Watchers, from their location in another dimension, notice the beauty of human women and experience desire for them. They generate the sexual act in their minds, and given that they have

---

*For an extensive discussion of the Watchers, sons of God, and Nephilim, see John J. Collins, "The Sons of God and the Daughters of Men," in Nissinen and Uro, *Sacred Marriages*, 259–74. Sexual encounters between humans and nonembodied beings are attested to worldwide; see, for example, Lewis, *Ecstatic Religion*, 57–64.

advanced powers, they change form so that they look like human males. They then insert themselves into the imaginations of certain women as they are having sex with their husbands so that the women find themselves fantasizing about engaging with these imaginary beings instead. That process is apparently so powerful that it results in women conceiving the children of the Watchers rather than those of their human partners. By getting mixed up with the sexual energy of humans, the Watchers can therefore install themselves on the earth plane. But they do leave a telltale sign of their shenanigans with the ladies: the children produced by their impregnations are as gigantic as they are.

Whether you personally take any of this to be real or not, this excerpt shows us that the idea that women could consort sexually with other nonhuman beings to the point of being impregnated by them was indeed alive and well in the ancient world.

THE RISE AND FALL OF DIVINE BIRTH THROUGH TIME

Over time in the ancient world, the methods that divine-birth priestesses used to spur conception shifted. In what follows, I lead you through that strange migration, a devolutionary process in which women were successively disempowered as the patriarchy took over.* This is important background for understanding what processes Mary; her mother, Anne; their relative Elizabeth; and their ancestor Sarah may have used to miraculously conceive children.

Bringing Forth Divine Daughters

The earliest practice of priestesses devoted to divine birth was a kind of holy parthenogenesis. This would be the method used by the Muse on the mountain, from the Nag Hammadi text that we looked at earlier. It involved the priestess entering into a special, spiritually infused erotic encounter with herself to spark the conception of a child. An encounter like this would have been no mere self-pleasuring episode. It would have

---

*This subject is explored in depth in my book *The Cult of Divine Birth in Ancient Greece*.

been a ritual that was deeply informed by the priestess's special understanding of how to work with her body, mind, and spirit. Such ancient knowledge was likely transmitted to her from the circle of priestesses to which she belonged, and after a long and deep process of apprenticeship.

The earliest form of this kind of spiritualized parthenogenetic practice would have led to the conception of female children. That's because technically and scientifically, if a woman self-conceives she will naturally give birth to a girl due to the fact that her eggs contain only X (female) chromosomes. The resulting child is not identical to her, because there is a different combination of her DNA in each egg. But nevertheless, a girl baby divinely conceived is viewed as being her "twin."

The holy parthenogenetic woman produced what amounted to the next female representation of the Divine Feminine on Earth. Hers was a very high-order daughter, who herself would become fully divine upon her own ritual death. It is likely this exalted daughter also served as a priestess or queen in her lifetime, and it may be that she engaged in the practice of divine birth as well.

I believe that in regions of Europe and North Africa, women who practiced sacred parthenogenesis in this way were following their divine role models; namely, goddesses who were originally virgin mothers, such as Gaia, Athena, Hera, and Artemis. The concept of mother-daughter "twins" also finds its cosmic parallel in the story of Demeter and Persephone. I see evidence that Demeter's conception of Persephone was originally a story of self-replication, and not the result of her impregnation by the god Zeus.*

It's important to bookmark this idea because this mother-daughter twinning process is precisely what we'll be looking at when we explore the story of Mary's own miraculous conception by her mother, Anne.

Bringing Forth Divine Sons

Holy parthenogenesis then moved into a second stage, in which women self-conceived male children. We see this in the case of the Muse on

---

*See an extensive discussion of this in my book *Virgin Mother Goddesses of Antiquity*, 103–7.

the mountain whose parthenogenetic encounter in fact resulted in the birth of a boy. This may have required the woman to work at additional sophisticated levels to adjust the chromosomal X into a Y. Symbolically, the process affirmed that the male was contained within the female rather than being something separate from her.

One of the ancient cosmic models for this kind of divine birth was Hera's parthenogenetic birth of Ares, Typhon, and Hephaistos. I believe Mary was engaged in this level of son-producing parthenogenesis, as was possibly the biblical Sarah before her, as we will see in the coming chapters. The holy male born this way became a king. According to the ancient Greek writer Pindar, the death of such a king was considered a "requital for [an] ancient wrong."[5] In other words, such a divinely born king would die to remedy the people's errors. This is precisely what happened in the case of Jesus, but it appears that this practice actually predates Jesus.

Sacred Marriages with Male Gods

With the rise of the patriarchy, further and more dramatic shifts took place in the methods that divine-birth priestesses used. We next see it in the emergence of the practice of sacred marriage. This was initially a rite that took place between a human priestess and a male god in the spirit realm. It resulted in the conception and birth of such a divinely co-conceived child.

Ancient Greek stories speak of maidens being "raped" by male gods, a continuation of the divine-conception theme. I propose that these stories are actually describing a process whereby a young priestess's holy parthenogenetic ritual is interrupted by a male god on the inner planes. Like the Watchers, these gods—that is, astral beings of some kind—had specific powers that allowed them to insert themselves into a priestess's imagination during the rite. They could then take over the proceedings and create an actual impregnation within her. In other words, a priestess's ritual to create her own self-conceived child could be co-opted by an interdimensional male nonhuman being. A male child was usually the result of such an act, although not always.

At first, divine-birth priestesses experienced these paranormal visitations as rapes, and therefore they resisted. But with the creeping development of patriarchy and the increasing pressure on these sacred women to conform to a new paradigm, the priestesses gradually began to consciously cultivate these extrahuman visitations. Such women would of course receive all the benefits of divine conception, such as a higher social status and even divinization for themselves and their offspring. But at the same time, by doing so they were conceding to the advancing patriarchy by bringing forth the sons of the patriarchal gods. And these divinely conceived sons were regarded as heroes who would then go about dismantling the remaining Mother-centered culture and women's spiritual authority.

Some of the mythological women who we are told were abducted by male gods for such purposes were Daphne, who was raped by Apollo; Syrinx, who was raped by Pan; Europa, who was raped by Zeus; and many others. Among these women are also several priestesses of legend, such as Aethra, the mother of Theseus; Danaë, the mother of Perseus; and Alcmene, the mother of Heracles. I believe that these so-called myths and legends are describing not fictional stories, but actual historical events.

In addition, it may surprise you to know that we have a number of women who are historically credited with having conceived children through unions with male gods. Among them are Olympias, the mother of Alexander the (so-called) Great, who willingly engaged in a sexual encounter with Zeus in his Egyptian form of Amun (just as the Egyptian queens did) to bring forth her son, Alexander. Later, in Rome, Atia, the daughter of Julius Caesar's sister, was said to have consorted with Apollo, leading to the birth of Augustus Caesar.[6]

Although men born this way often began a rampage to dismantle women's rights, rituals, and roles—witness Heracles, Theseus, and Perseus especially—not all sons born of priestesses' liaisons with gods were negative forces on the planet. Plato and Pythagoras, for example, were said to have been divinely conceived by their mothers, Perictione and Pythias respectively, through their unions with Apollo. Clearly these men brought great benefit to humanity.

I believe that the quality of the divinely born son depended on the level of integrity and true spiritual advancement of the priestess herself. This is something we will see dramatically played out in the case of Mary, one of the most advanced souls who ever graced the planet.

Male God Stand-Ins Enter the Picture

In yet a later phase of the practice of divine conception, a human stand-in substituted for a god in the sacred marriage rite. This male actor was usually a priest-king who himself was divinely born. The process of procreation involved him basically getting out of the way so that the spirit of a god could enter his body during the sex act, leading to the conception of a child considered to be in the god's lineage. This is how some of the Egyptian pharaohs were born, starting as early as 3000 BCE. We see in ancient poetry and artwork strong suggestions that priestesses and priest-kings enacted such rituals in Sumer (ancient Iraq) and basically everywhere in the ancient Near East, including Syria, Canaan, and the southern Levant, going back as early as 2700 BCE.* As we will see, elements of this practice seem to poke through in Sarah's relationship with Abraham, and even in Anne's relationship with her partner, Joachim.

I also have detected an intermediary step between male-producing parthenogenesis and strict male stand-in practice. This involved the priestess's use of an artificial phallus—a holy dildo—in her divine-birth rites. As I write in *The Cult of Divine Birth in Ancient Greece* and *Virgin Mother Goddesses of Antiquity*, these erotic implements peskily appear in ancient religious writings, a fact that has caused most scholars to turn away in embarrassment. But I believe they were ritually used in ways that show that the ancient Greeks and Egyptians connected holiness and sexuality in quite graphic ways.

---

*For a historical and symbolic perspective of sacred marriage in the ancient Near East as well as in Greco-Roman mystery religion sources, gnostic material, medieval Jewish mysticism, and more, see Nissinen and Uro, *Sacred Marriages: The Divine-Human Sexual Metaphor from Sumer to Early Christianity*. Bewilderingly, most scholars dismiss the idea that sacred marriage rites included sexual intercourse. I find this strange given what to me seems to be overwhelming evidence to the contrary. I contend that my research, by providing a more comprehensive theoretical context as to what was going on and why, further moves the needle in the direction of our understanding that sex was indeed part of such rites.

The most dramatic example of the use of a holy dildo in association with a divine conception can be found in the story of the Egyptian goddess Isis. We hear that after her brother Osiris is dismembered by her other, jealous brother, Seth, Isis must gather his body parts in order to put him back together so that she can become pregnant by him posthumously. She finds everything except his phallus. This leads her to render him a new one, and it is through her activity with this phallus that she is able to become pregnant with her son, Horus. Voilà, the dildo of Isis!

It is very likely that this story is not merely mythological, but that it is rather describing an actual historical event. According to Plutarch's *On Isis and Osiris* (27/361E), Isis is said to have been elevated from the status of a semidivine being to the rank of full divinity.[7] Given ancient beliefs that the gods of old actually walked the planet as humans who possessed extraordinary powers—something we will see play out with the entire Holy Family—we can take the story of Isis and her encounters with Osiris as describing a very high-level woman. Her rising to the level of divinity was probably the result of her miraculous impregnation by Osiris, an idea consistent with what I have discovered about all such divine-birth priestesses. This is why she is now thought of as a goddess.

With the male stand-in practice of divine birth, a significant change took place in priestesses' authority and rights. Given that a human male was now physically involved in the practice, the divinely born child that resulted could now be claimed by a male line. This contrasts with earlier matrilineal tradition, wherein the priestess was the sovereign actor and she could therefore take credit for, and take charge of, the child. With this change, the tradition of the divine-birth priestesshood became completely absorbed by the patriarchy. Holy parthenogenetic women no longer had exclusive claim to their children, and therefore no longer had the social status and rights they once had.

OKAY . . . BUT WHY VIRGINITY?

A number of conditions were necessary for divine conception to happen, and one was that the woman involved had to be a virgin, or at the very least she had to be celibate for the duration of the divine-conception practice. Why? Because celibacy allowed for the storing up of her vital sexual energies so that she would have the necessary voltage for the task. Having sexual relations with a man would dissipate that energy, whereas engaging in parthenogenesis or sex with a disembodied being would not.

I found a relevant term in Greek that is worth mentioning here, *parthénos,* the root word of parthenogenesis. While this word is often used to simply describe a young unmarried girl or virgin, it also has a more complex meaning. Sometimes it refers to a woman who had sexual relations with gods or who gave birth to the children of gods—and such a woman was not necessarily young. A related term, *paida,* is also sometimes translated as "girl," but also has a deeper sacred meaning, as we see when this word is applied to Mary. In the New Testament, Mary is referred to as a parthénos, as are a number of divine-birth priestesses in ancient Greece. I therefore believe that the word *parthénos* (*parthénoi* in the plural) was often a title for a divine-birth priestess.

Youth was an ideal precondition for a female entering a divine-birth priestesshood, although it was not an absolute requirement. We find in the Greek stories that the majority of holy parthénoi were girls in early puberty; however, the main exceptions to this are found outside Greece, in the Hebrew tradition. Here, for example, we hear of the miraculous conception of Isaac by the elderly matriarch Sarah, which I will discuss in chapter 4. As well, Mary's mother, Anne, was also past normal biological childbearing age when she conceived Mary, as was Mary's relative Elizabeth when she brought forth her son, John the Baptist.

"HIGH" PRIESTESSES: ALTERED STATES AND PLANT MEDICINE

In my explorations I have found clues that these women may have engaged in the practice of divine conception by first entering a profound trance state. Again, this brings us back to the oracular Muse who sits on the mountain and enters into a deep state of meditation. We see hints in the ancient texts that the proper open state of consciousness may have been generated by priestesses' use of psychoactive plant medicines.

Not surprisingly, then, divine-birth priestesses were therefore also oracular priestesses—that is, they possessed psychic and prophetic abilities. Obviously, their natural talents combined with their intensely specialized training opened all of their spiritual capabilities to a very high level. We see this most clearly in the case of the priestesses who served at the great Greek oracle center of Delphi. There, sacred women entered into trance states and uttered the words of the divine realms for their clients. We know that many of the original priestesses associated with Delphi, such as Corycia, Celaeno, and Thyia, are credited with giving birth to children of the god Apollo. As we shall see, this dual role of oracle and divine conceiver is also true in the case of the Hebrew women Sarah, Anne, and Mary.

The concept of receiving children into the womb and receiving inspired ideas in the mind is reflected in the English verb *to conceive,* and in the ancient Greek verb *anaireô.* The Greek term has three meanings: "to give an oracle," "to take up," and "to conceive in the womb." In other words, it can be translated as "receiving children into the womb" and as "receiving inspired ideas in the mind" (giving oracles and prophecy). But it is the third meaning, "to take up," that provides a link between the two other translations and shows how prophecy and divine conception were both part of the same territory.

Anaireô was specifically used to describe how the Delphic priestesses delivered Apollo's oracles. The "taking up" part of its meaning is reflected in the fact that these priestesses were believed to literally take up or absorb certain chemical vapors through the vagina.* They would do so by squatting over a chasm in the earth, out of which such naturally arising earthly gases would enter into the tissue of their vaginas and, from there, spread into their bloodstream. The chemicals in the fumes would then stimulate in them the precise open state of consciousness needed for the encounter with divine intelligence that spurred prophecy. Thus, this "taking up" was seen as the way the god's inspiration entered the priestess; moreover, it was considered a form of sexual intercourse because it took place in the woman's vagina—and, I would

---

*For more on this, see my book *The Cult of Divine Birth in Ancient Greece,* 180–85.

add, because it also generated a profound erotic feeling in the woman, something I personally have experienced in my own ceremonies using sacred medicine.

At Delphi, sometimes this process of "taking up" the god resulted in inspired prophecy, and sometimes it resulted in the woman's literally conceiving a child of the god. We know this because many of the legends and place names associated with Delphi bear the names of the priestesses who either bore children by virtue of a sexual relationship with the god Apollo or who actively resisted his advances to avoid impregnation.

The multiple meanings of conception as found in the word *anaireô* also indicate that the ancient Greeks understood the relationship between the womb and what Plato refers to in his writings as the "third eye." In contemporary spiritual thought the third eye corresponds to the pituitary gland behind the forehead and is considered the organ by which one receives oracular information. The energetic connection between these two regions of the female body, the third eye and the womb, further explains why prophetesses could be both oracles and parthenogenetic priestesses, for the gifts of the gods, delivered in the form of either divine oracular knowledge or human souls, were all a part of the same interdimensional territory. I believe that the literal conception of a divine child was considered the highest level of oracle practice.

SELF-LOVE: THE DESIRE FOR DESIRE

That virginity or chastity was required for the successful accomplishment of divine birth doesn't mean the process involved the stifling of erotic feelings. Quite the contrary. This is perhaps more obvious in the case of priestesses who engaged in sexual relations with gods. But even in cases such as that of the parthenogenetic Muse on the mountain, we can see that the work of self-conception was a highly erotic act. Such a woman, as we saw, had to bring desire into the equation in order to stimulate the needed energies.

In the ancient world, an altered state of consciousness was often called "ecstasy." This is precisely because it led a person to union with the Divine, which was generally felt to be extremely pleasurable, even sexual in nature. Anyone who has entered a level of consciousness brought about by deep meditation or entheogenic plant medicine will understand this. We learned from the Muse on the mountain that divine-birth priestesses were specifically required to cultivate the erotic aspect of this experience, so desire was a key ingredient, as sacred conception united carnal sexuality with elevated spiritual consciousness. The women who engaged with their own divine goddess selves through sacred parthenogenesis experienced a profound erotic merging with the All That Is. This put them in touch with what I call the sexual nature of the universe as Creatrix. It was only when they achieved this apex, which culminated in orgasm, that the conception would take place. And priestesses who united sexually with gods or with males who embodied gods were engaged in eroticism even more obviously.

It may be useful to call to mind Teresa of Ávila's mystical encounters. In her writings she describes her unification with the Divine as a profound kind of pain/pleasure (one that was aptly captured by Bernini in his famous erotic sculpture *Ecstasy of Saint Teresa*). We should note, however, that by the time the cohorts of priestesses gave way to the nunneries of the Catholic Church, knowledge of divine conception had been erased. So while a woman like Teresa could experience the throes of ecstasy in her religious raptures, she no longer possessed the technology to create a divine conception out of such an experience. Entering into altered states of consciousness was generally considered a suspicious activity or was completely taboo in the Christian establishment (witness the struggles of Joan of Arc, who was martyred, and Hildegard of Bingen, who in her eighties had to face down an interdict against her, for example), which means that Teresa was riding a very dangerous line in revealing her mystical experiences of merging with the Divine. We will see how the practice of uniting with Divine Feminine Creator was indeed part of Mother Mary's work to bring in Jesus later in the book.

OTHER FACETS OF DIVINE-BIRTH PRIESTESSHOODS

Transmission through Lineages

Often the practice of divine birth was passed down in families. I have found various examples of this in ancient writings regarding mother-daughter and matriarchal lineages. This was the case with Mary; her mother, Anne; and her relative Elizabeth. I believe these women transferred their knowledge from generation to generation. What I have also come to understand is that priestesses in some cases practiced divine birth as part of a group ritual. In fact, such women would sometimes attempt the practice together in a single ritual, something that we see in the gospel dealing with Mary's birth and childhood. It appears that the women who did not conceive after such a ritual would become part of the "nurse" contingent that would raise the child.

Communing with Stars and Conceiving with Light

We also see that divine-birth priestesses were often linked in some way to the stars. A number of them had names or gave names to their divinely born children that were linguistically related to *astér,* the Greek word for "star." This tells us that they had a profound understanding of our connection to what Native Americans call "star beings." Native lore says that these beings are ancestors of humanity who still operate in more elevated ways than we presently do on Planet Earth. Indeed, there is much to indicate that divine-birth priestesses were calling to their wombs helpful souls from these more advanced star intelligences.

As we will see, Mary herself came to be identified with the stars in one of her titles, Stella Maris, meaning "Star of the Sea." In addition, the birth of Jesus was accompanied by the appearance of a certain bright star. All of this suggests that Mary, too, was working with the domain of star beings in her conception of Jesus.

Various ancient texts describe the reception of a divine soul occurring through a "flash of light" from either the heavens or the moon.[8] In Egypt, one ambiguous spell found in the Coffin Texts may indicate that Isis was impregnated by a flash of lightning.[9] A number of famous artists have perhaps intuited this ancient understanding by depicting Mary's conception of Jesus as taking place through a ray of light penetrating her womb. Clairvoyant author Claire Heartsong has verified this idea independently in her noteworthy channeled work *Anna, Grandmother of Jesus,* wherein she reports being shown that the kind of divine pregnancies that Mary's lineage was capable of were called light conceptions—that is, they required the priestesses to engage with divine light on the quantum level in order to conceive parthenogenetically.[10]

I would like to bring into the discussion a far more recent example of what appears to have been a light conception. This not only verifies the concept, it also shows us that the practice of divine birth never fully disappeared. In his book *Parthenogenesis: Women's Long-Lost Ability to Self-Conceive,* author Den Poitras tells the story of his good friend, pseudonymously named Laurie, who spontaneously conceived a child on the evening of December 24, 1976, after several years of intense spiritual practice. Laurie called him that night, breathless with excitement, and told him, "I've just had an incredible experience with a powerful light, a blissful light. And while within this state of bliss I was told that I had conceived a child!"[11] Amazingly, Laurie's pregnancy was verified medically in the months following the conception and was honored as a sacred planetary event by a Hopi elder to whom she was synchronistically led in Arizona. According to Poitras, Laurie did indeed carry her child to term, although it lived only three months. I possess the original (and quite fascinating) letters that Laurie wrote to Poitras detailing some of the events around her pregnancy, and I have no reason to doubt her claim.*

Flying with the Doves

Another symbol we see associated with divine-birth priestesses is the dove, a bird associated with the group of stars known as the Pleiades. The female beings called the Seven Sisters of the Pleiades were consid-

---

*I have attempted to contact Laurie myself, but she has not returned my communications. Poitras, who affirms that she is a woman of integrity who would not have fabricated her story, informs me that she told him the entire episode brings up painful memories that she would rather not relive by discussing it. I respect her privacy around this.

ered by the Greeks and many others around the world to be the mothers of humanity by virtue of having conceived key lineages as a result of their sexual relations with gods. These sisters, also referred to as the "seven doves," were virgins. The symbol of the dove appears in relation to Mary as well, as we will see in chapter 5.

Weaving Reality into Being

We see in the ancient writings that divine birth is often associated with weaving. Weaving is a symbol of parthenogenesis in part because it represents the process of creation by a single woman who draws threads together to manifest something out of thin air. This connection is found strongly in one of the earliest known goddesses of ancient Egypt, Neith, the goddess of weaving, who was said to have created herself out of the void. In other words, Neith was parthenogenetic to a very high degree in that she was nothing less than autogenetic, or self-generating.

In ancient Greece, the weaving of the sacred dress of the Goddess to adorn her statues in the temples was a very great and important rite. The weaving motif also appears in relation to Mary, who is engaged in weaving the temple veil when she conceives Jesus. The Sanskrit word *tantra,* taken from *tanoti,* translates as "to weave together," so the inner tantra that I talked about earlier regarding the Muse on the mountain has to do with parthenogenesis as an inner erotic weaving.

Eating Just Right

In my travels since my first two books were published, I have been persuaded by information suggesting that divine-birth priestesses had to purify themselves physically in order to conceive in a different way, and this involved a special diet. There are several intriguing contemporary claims that support this idea. One comes from the prolific esoteric writer Raymond W. Bernard,* who wrote that parthenogenetic

---

*Raymond W. Bernard was the pen name of Walter Siegmeister (1903–1965). He also wrote under the names Dr. Robert Raymond and Dr. Uriel Adriana. He held an MA from Columbia and a PhD from New York University, and was influenced by the work of Rudolf Steiner. For more on Bernard, see resources in the Wikipedia entry.

conception *can* occur, but it requires the cessation of the menses. He further supplied the means by which menstruation can be stopped: by turning to a strict diet of only uncooked vegetables, wearing loose clothing, and abstaining from sexual intercourse.[12] What I've come to understand is that the cessation of the menses is not the goal here; it's simply the by-product of the physical purification that occurs when women ingest only high-quality vegan food and purify their bodies regularly through fasting.

A second claim comes from metaphysical teacher and historian Dr. Delbert Blair (d. 2016). In his various lectures, many of which are available online as videos, he asserts that women can reproduce parthenogenetically, and he similarly refers to a vegetarian diet to accomplish this, which can lead to the cessation of menstruation.[13] Given the similarities between Blair's claims and Bernard's written works, Blair may be drawing from the books of the latter.

The third claim relevant here is that of Laurie, mentioned earlier, who reported her miraculous conception in 1976, when she was twenty years old. Writing about this dramatic event, Poitras reports that prior to her spontaneous pregnancy, Laurie had been celibate for years and had lived for more than a year on only water, or water mixed with a very finely strained juice made from grapes. All the while she maintained her natural body weight (in other words she was not anorexic). She was able to live as a "breatharian" in this way by being intensely connected to the world of spirit, which fed her in deeper ways.

I also want to bring into this discussion a holy woman I know well, named Angela de la Agua. Part of Angela's spiritual practice involves eating a vegan or plant-based diet, with an emphasis on raw foods and very simple eating. She works with food very mindfully, considers it a sacrament, and regularly fasts for periods of three to 120 days. Her practice includes yearly five-day vision quests in the wild desert lands where she lives with no food or water. What Angela has told me confirms the relationship between bodily purification and menstruation: "Going on extended fasting eliminates my womb's need to cleanse," she says, "and I have gone up to eight months without having my menses cycle. Once I begin eating again, after a month or two, the cycle returns." Like

Laurie, Angela is also able to maintain a healthy body weight throughout her fasts. And again, that is because physical food is not her only form of nourishment.

Angela has deliberately engaged in periods of celibacy that have lasted years, and she naturally wears flowing clothing. About her practices, she says: "While I have not attempted parthenogenesis, from the moment the concept entered my awareness it activated a hidden truth within me. I suddenly realized there was a greater purpose to my path and why I've been guided to live the way I do. I saw that I'd been led to undergo years of initiations to prepare myself for this level of divine service to the world. As the journey evolves, I hold an expansive awareness of how 'divine birth' may be interpreted and achieved in my unique path."

Angela's dietary practices leading to the natural and problem-free cessation of menstruation, and Laurie's remarkable experience of spontaneous pregnancy after a period of celibacy and fasting, bring to mind two references in Mary's infancy gospel. These, as we will see, allude to the possibility that Mary was on a special diet for her entire young life as part of her training for sacred parthenogenesis. Laurie and Angela's stories not only help us understand Mary's past, they also open the door to the future of divine birth.

THE DEATH AND REBIRTH OF DIVINE BIRTH

What we've looked at in this chapter gives us some of the history as well as the key signs, symbols, and significators of what I interchangeably call *miraculous conception, virgin birth,* and *divine birth.*

The trajectory of divine birth that I have shared stops at the point where priestesses' conception rites were completely taken over by male priest-kings, who then claimed the divinely born children for the male line. But there is more to the story. In the centuries following that development, divine-birth priestesshoods were prevented from giving birth altogether. The women involved were required to remain virgins, while their womb energy was siphoned off to fuel patriarchal institutions—a subject we'll look at more closely in the story of the

Hebrew matriarch Sarah in chapter 4, and the Vestal Virgins in chapter 5.

In Western Europe, eventually these powerful virgin cohorts degenerated even further as the women were stripped of any knowledge of their miraculous reproductive power. Virgin birth met its dead end in the various celibate nunhoods, where holy women were denied not only their womb knowing, but also nearly all of the privileges and status their lineages once held. Eventually patriarchy in the form of science totally obliterated the concept of divine birth by telling us that miraculous conception was a complete physical impossibility. And where it remained a religious concept, it was stripped of its connection to women's wisdom, spiritual power, sacred technologies, and history, making it a metaphor at best. Virgin birth thus became something that people had to take on pure faith if they were going to consider it at all. As a result, thinking people rejected the idea. And where miraculous conception or divine birth remained a living practice, it had to be veiled in secrecy. This is in part because negative occult powers were keen to sniff it out and eradicate it whenever possible.

All of this means that the present discussion of divine birth is a great unveiling taking place in our time. What we have looked at in this chapter will allow us to not only make sense of Mary's story at long last, but also to consider what powers women are still capable of. Laurie and Angela are not the only women I have known personally who have been drawn to the practice of divine birth in our time. I know of others, some of whom have indeed conceived children through miraculous means, and all of whom have fascinating stories. I am constantly astounded by sharings that women bring to me regarding other details of their pregnancies that cannot be explained through ordinary means. And from time to time I hear from women who have had unusual sexual encounters on the spirit plane. All of this points to a miraculous conception tradition that is not a dead artifact of the long-ago past, but a living reality.

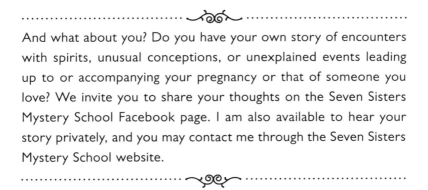

And what about you? Do you have your own story of encounters with spirits, unusual conceptions, or unexplained events leading up to or accompanying your pregnancy or that of someone you love? We invite you to share your thoughts on the Seven Sisters Mystery School Facebook page. I am also available to hear your story privately, and you may contact me through the Seven Sisters Mystery School website.

May our exploration of Mary and the divine-birth mysteries of the past give women throughout the globe a better understanding of the true nature of feminine energy so that we may together (pro)create an evolutionary future.

CHAPTER 3

Uncovering the Jewel of Mother Mary's Suppressed Gospel

Who was Mary, the mother of Jesus, really? We get mere tidbits about her in the New Testament gospels, particularly Matthew and Luke, and that's about it. So we must go beyond the Bible to get any significant information about the world's most famous holy woman.

What may surprise you is that Mary is actually mentioned in the Islamic Qur'an more often than she is in the New Testament. In that Muslim sacred text, two of the longer chapters are devoted to Mary and her family. The narratives there honor her as the greatest of all women, one who was surrounded by divine grace from birth and who was chosen as a virgin by God for the miraculous conception of Jesus.*

But there is more. Most people do not realize that one of the best and most detailed sources of information about Mary is neither the New Testament nor the Qur'an, but another historical document, a text that has rather drearily come to be called the Infancy Gospel of James, also known as the Protevangelium of James. Since it is this apocryphal gospel on which my sleuthing into the subject of this book is based, I give you here a brief introduction to it so that you know what you're dealing with. We'll look at the gospel's history: its original name, its dating and

---

*For good consolidated references, see the Wikipedia entries "Mary in Islam" and "Maryam (surah)."

authorship, and its suppression, along with other texts that were rejected by the Catholic Church. We'll also explore evidence for its authenticity despite the fact that it was officially edited out of the Christian canon, as well as what I believe is its mystical and inspired nature.

THE SUPPRESSION OF MOTHER MARY'S GOSPEL

The oldest manuscript of the Infancy Gospel of James now available is called the Bodmer papyrus, which was unearthed in the sands of Egypt in the early twentieth century and published in 1958. It dates back to the early fourth century, but the original text was probably written much earlier. The original manuscript bears a different and much more accurate title: Birth of Mary, Revelation of James. And according to some scholars, only the first half of that title is likely to have been the actual name of this gospel, which leaves us with Birth of Mary as the original name of this text.[1]

The Birth of Mary—such a title strikes me as much more apt, because, well, the gospel is entirely about Mary's early life! In the sixth century, the Birth of Mary did not make the cut when the Catholic Church declared which books would be considered canonical; that is, the officially designated divine scriptures of the Bible. The lineup of what was to be considered acceptable by the Church was issued in its Gelasian Decree, which threw this gospel on the Catholic Church's rubbish heap, along with other Apocrypha; that is, early Christian writings that were considered to be heretical. The Latin Catholic priest Jerome even said this gospel was "full of absurdities" because of its claim that Joseph had sons by a previous marriage, and popes Damasus, Innocent I, and Gelasius I also dismissed it as untrustworthy.[2]

This extreme response should be a clue for us. In my view, the Apocrypha are full of information that was suppressed because it threatened the Church's patriarchal dogma and unchallenged civil authority. I am one of many people who find this body of rejected material, along with other suppressed writings sometimes referred to as "gnostic," to be full of important spiritual truths and some of the most fascinating historical information in the entire library of Christian works. From this perspective, that the Birth of Mary was placed in the category of the Apocrypha is actually a very good thing; it tells us that we should take a close look at it.

Some churches must have felt similarly, because while the West rejected this important gospel, the Byzantine East embraced it, even including it in their masses.[3] And curiously, despite its supposed absurdities, the Roman Catholic Church drew on its stories to establish various holy days that honor events in the life of Mary, such as the Immaculate Conception on December 8, which essentially marks her conception by Anne; her birth on September 8; her "presentation in the temple" on November 21 (I always used to wonder, *Huh? What presentation?*); and the "visitation" between Mary and Elizabeth on May 31.

Despite its suppression by the Church, the people always held this gospel close. As cultural historian Ally Kateusz has discovered, that this gospel was early on considered scripture is confirmed by the fact that some of its stories appear in the oldest surviving Christian art.[4] Later artists such as da Vinci and Titian were also inspired by this text, taking its descriptions of the people and events in Mary's life and depicting them on canvases and church walls.

Nevertheless, in Medieval and Renaissance Europe the Birth of Mary fell off the map until 1552, when someone decided to pull it out of obscurity, translate it into Latin from an older (now lost) Greek version, and publish it. Bravo—but apparently that person also gave this gospel its current boring and meaningless title, which unfortunately is the one that has stuck. Scholars obstinately continue to use the nondescriptive name that puts the spotlight on its author and leaves its protagonist, Mary, in the dark. Throughout the rest of this book I will not make that same mistake. I will steadfastly refer to this gospel by the earliest title we have for it, the Birth of Mary.*

---

*Bear in mind that you are not likely to see it referred to by its original title until the movement to uncover the truth about Mary takes hold, so if you would like to find out more about this early Christian work, check it out under its original name, Infancy Gospel of James, aka Protevangelium of James.

HOW RELIABLE IS THIS GOSPEL?

The author of the Birth of Mary supposedly is someone named James. This may actually be one of the children of Joseph, who this gospel claims was born to him through a marriage he had prior to his guardianship of Mary. We clearly note that in another apocryphal text, the Infancy Gospel of Thomas (16:1), one of Joseph's sons is indeed named James. This would make him the older stepbrother of Jesus.

Others think that this James is the one who Matthew (13:55–56) states was a brother of Jesus, a reference that some have taken to mean he was a full blood brother born of Mary after she gave birth to Jesus. Either identification places him very close in time to many of the events recounted in this gospel. If he was indeed the older stepbrother of Jesus, alive when Mary came into his father Joseph's fold, he was an eyewitness to certain events described in the gospel.

This author, James, also claimed to be writing the text shortly after the death of Herod, which would date the writing to 4 BCE, commonly considered to be the time of the birth of Jesus and John the Baptist. If indeed the text dates anywhere near 4 BCE, this would make it extremely important because that means it precedes even the earliest writings of the New Testament by more than fifty years. This makes it a font of critical information about Mary herself; her mother, Anne; her relative Elizabeth; how Jesus and John the Baptist came to be; and various other events that took place around this Holy Family.

Most scholars and theologians, however, reject the idea that the author could have been related to Jesus and dismiss the author's claim of the date of his writing. In assessing these arguments from my own background as a scholar of religion, I am not convinced by them, but I will not go into an analysis of why here, as this has in part been taken up by other scholars.* I will, however, say that part of the issue, as I see it, is that most academics approach the text from what amounts to an embedded bias that anything outside the canonical texts must have been based on the New Testament gospels as their

---

*See, for example, Hock, 8–13 and 21–27, for a detailed discussion of these arguments.

primary source material. They inevitably begin their analyses from this often subtly held viewpoint, thus continuing the abuses of the Gelasian Decree that dismissed all the early material as inauthentic. Scholars assume, therefore, that the Birth of Mary must have been written *after* Matthew and Luke, in more like the second century CE, around 150 CE at the earliest.

What's more, in dating it thus they imply that much of what the text contains is charmingly fictional, retroactively made up to provide support for the Church's agenda regarding the veneration of Mary. I don't find their theories about the dating particularly convincing, however. The inconsistencies or textual problems the Church points to concerning this gospel do not seem alarming enough to invalidate it as an authentic source, and I believe that many of these issues could be explained in other ways. In fact, this manuscript, like the other Apochrypha, bears evidence of having been tampered with by later church scribes, who copied it by hand. So it may be that some of the debated issues stem from those transcriptions.

The Birth of Mary has also been trounced for supposedly containing cultural practices that never existed in the Hebrew tradition, specifically as regards women. This viewpoint says that the gospel must have been fabricated by a zealous Christian author who wished to "read back" Christian customs into the past. But Ally Kateusz states that "[r]ecent research demonstrates that although some of this author's descriptions of Jewish customs are not what we might expect given scripture . . . they nonetheless were consistent with Jewish custom as told in the Mishnah and other Jewish texts of that era."[5] I will bring to light some of these intriguing customs in the coming chapters.

In addition, we find that some of the gospel's storyline has been validated—and even added to—by the Qur'an and other early Islamic authorities, as we will see later.* So the Birth of Mary is hardly a stand-alone romance novel, as the Church suggests, but rather a popular text that was considered important by various religious authorities until the early centuries of the Common Era. Its themes and story line

---

*See, for example, Qur'an 19.

appear in works by other authors who wrote later apocryphal texts about Mary.

THE MYSTICAL NATURE OF MARY'S GOSPEL

Based on my research on divine-birth practices in the ancient world of Europe, the Middle East, and Africa, I find that the Birth of Mary is chock-full of remarkable correspondences to what I have proposed in my previous books, in which I revealed the existence of an entire program of women's sacred practices of divine conception in the ancient Western world. The many details that Mary's gospel offers are so intricately and surprisingly related to what I have uncovered already that it could not possibly have been written by someone retroactively spinning a yarn for the sake of providing the Catholic Church either with more dogma or with an entertaining backstory about the main characters of Christianity to satisfy the masses. Nor is it likely to have been written by someone simply trying to make Mary look good. I believe that only an author who was telling the truth could have described the things we will see are unearthed in this gospel. In fact, I contend that the Birth of Mary conveys nothing less than the hidden history and secret mystery teachings of the early Christians.

It is a well-known adage that mystery-school teachings must be both revealed and concealed at the same time. This is partly because they can never be fully explained—verbally, anyway—as they can only be understood by direct experience. This is also because the mysteries contain tremendous power, a power that could be misused in the wrong hands. In addition, mystery teachings inevitably threaten the status quo of the patriarchy, and this was all the more the case during the time this gospel was written. Mystery knowledge was thus considered subversive and dangerous and put the lives of those involved in writing or perpetuating it at great risk. The dangers associated with telling the truth about the mysteries is related throughout this gospel by its author, who at the conclusion tells us he had to go into hiding to write it. As a result, the Birth of Mary contains what I call a double-toned narrative: On the one hand it boldly conveys the supernatural nature of the events at play.

On the other, it necessarily waters things down by portraying some of the characters (such as Anne and Joachim) as just regular folks dealing with prosaic human emotions and problems, rather than as the special holy people they were.

I believe the gospel's author manages this tension between the need to both reveal and conceal by dangling words, phrases, symbols, events, and concepts that can only be understood by initiates of certain mysteries. By uncovering the special meanings, I will reveal an alternative narrative going on beneath the surface, one in which the women are active priestesses of divine birth, and the main male actors are aware of this and support their work.

I believe the two-toned quality of this gospel, which serves to deflect attention away from its deeper meaning, is what in fact allowed it to survive for some two thousand years. Male church leaders dismissed it as absurd rather than as threatening, and aside from rejecting it as a legitimate church document they otherwise left it alone.* What I have received in my meditations is that many other narratives were not so lucky and were thus totally eradicated. Indeed, I subsequently have learned that history bears this out: in the fourth century CE, the Bishop of Athanasius of Alexandria ordered monks to destroy all texts not specifically designated as canonical.[6] We are therefore blessed that the author of the Birth of Mary was as crafty as he was in lowballing its contents.

Very important to this argument is Kateusz's documented discovery that later scribes actually edited out or changed key words or phrases attesting to Mary's power in numerous texts that depict her life and death.[7] The watering down of Mary's role has indeed been detected in the Birth of Mary, as successive generations of scribes (probably monks) had to find a way to contend with details that depicted her power, authority, and sovereignty—realities that were denied the official patriarchal permission slip.† It may be that later copyists deleted or replaced

---

*For an excellent discussion of how early Christian texts that contained signs of women's power were deliberately tampered with by later scribes or outright destroyed, see Kateusz, 184–90.

†See, for example, my discussion centering on the gospel's use of the word *throne* in chapter 6.

offending words and phrases that now we cannot even trace despite the most careful comparative analyses across various editions. That means they left plain only what they themselves did not understand and therefore did not find threatening. I propose that such possible scribal tampering may have further contributed to the two-toned quality of this gospel in places. And of course such tampering could be the cause of various inconsistencies and problems that have given pause to serious scholars assessing its dating and authenticity.

Despite whatever editing may have occurred, the hidden meanings contained within the Birth of Mary are still there, and they are extremely rich. I believe that the author was not only an eyewitness to some of the events recalled, he was a mystic well versed in the mystery teachings of women, in particular. It is the specific inclusion of such women's secrets, especially those related to divine conception, that makes this gospel quite unusual among the early Christian writings.

What we will find is that this gospel reveals powerful information about Mary and her family, information I believe to be reliable. My interpretation of these details further validates the gospel's authenticity. I also hold open the possibility that the claim of its author about its dating is valid, and that therefore this may well be one of our earliest existing Christian religious texts.

At least 140 full or partial manuscript versions in Greek of the Birth of Mary have been unearthed in Egypt and have been found peppered throughout European libraries since the mid-sixteenth century. Using the oldest version available from the fourth century CE as a base, modern scholars have since added fragments from other manuscripts, sometimes translating the text in different ways in an attempt to create a single definitive edition. A very comprehensive version of the gospel can be found in the edition annotated by religion scholar Ronald Hock (which is found in the appendix of this book).

Fans of Mary Magdalene will be interested to know that the Birth of Mary makes a beautiful companion piece to the Gospel of Mary (i.e., Mary Magdalene's gospel). That gospel, also suppressed for centuries, has in recent decades been dusted off and mined for its riches about the secret sacred life of its protagonist (and possibly author), whom scholars agree must be Magdalene. In it, this advanced female apostle reveals special teachings given only to her by Jesus. It also exposes the competition provoked by Peter, whose view of reality would establish the foundation for what eventually would become the mighty Roman Catholic Church.

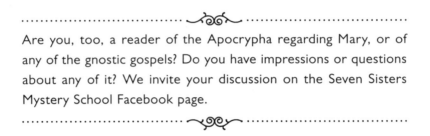

Are you, too, a reader of the Apocrypha regarding Mary, or of any of the gnostic gospels? Do you have impressions or questions about any of it? We invite your discussion on the Seven Sisters Mystery School Facebook page.

Whether the Birth of Mary was written in 4 BCE, the late second century CE, or some other time, it provides many more details about the life of Mary and early holy women's mystery practices than anyone has previously realized. By looking at this text in the next few chapters through the lens of my long-standing research into divine birth, a Mary never before seen—one who is the prime agent of Jesus's miraculous conception—will spring to life.

CHAPTER 4

Anne's Divine Conception of Mary

When I ask people whether they realize that Mary herself was divinely born just like Jesus, they generally respond with an incredulous "no" and want to know more. This chapter is that "more." We will dig into the Birth of Mary by first looking at what this intriguing gospel says about Mary's remarkable birth by her mother, Anne. We will learn that Anne and her consort, Joachim, are special holy people who held a very high status in their community. We will come to see how they supported each other spiritually in conceiving Mary, and we will uncover subtly veiled information about Anne's own process of divine birth. We will also take a good look at the biblical matriarch Sarah, wife of Abraham and mother of the miraculously conceived Isaac, to show that the divine-birth practice was going on in the Hebrew tradition from its inception.

WE START WITH JOACHIM

Mary's gospel begins by introducing us to Joachim, a standout person in the Hebrew community. Not only is he extremely holy, he is also wealthy and generous. He seems to have it all, but he has one problem: his companion, Anne, has not yet given birth to a child despite the fact that both of them are of advanced age.

Let's go to a telling scene. As a religious feast day approaches and the people of Israel are bringing their offerings to the temple, a self-designated temple bouncer named Reubel stands in Joachim's way. He announces that it is inappropriate for Joachim to offer his gifts first if he has not had any children. This puts Joachim into something of a tailspin. He calls to mind the patriarch Abraham's similar situation, knowing that God can provide miracles such as he did with the birth of Isaac when Abraham's wife, Sarah, was, like his own wife, Anne, past traditional childbearing years. Are he and his wife to be in that same lineage of miraculous birth, he wonders?

To get an answer to his question, he decides to leave for the wilderness, pitch his tent, and fast for forty days and forty nights. He declares that the constant refrain in his heart will be: "I will not go down for food or drink until the Lord my God visits me; prayer will be my food and drink."

What's happening here? Joachim is embarking on what we might call a classic vision quest; that is, a spiritual journey in which bodily deprivation is intended to send him into an altered, open state of consciousness. It seems clear that like most people who have engaged in vision quests, he is hoping this process will allow him to connect with the divine realms and receive guidance. We can imagine that at that time, as is the case now, this kind of extreme vision questing was not something taken up lightly. That Joaquim knows he can access divine information suggests he is not your average Joe, but is rather a deeply spiritual man in Israelite society. A fast of forty days and forty nights in the wilderness is a spiritual theme we see elsewhere in the Hebrew Bible,* and this incident foreshadows a similar fast that Jesus will later observe.

This journey therefore puts Joachim on the same level as the most elevated seekers and seers of his time. His wealth indicates that he also has high social status; we hear in the gospel that he always doubles his temple gifts, one part being for the community and the other being a means of atoning for any wrongdoing he has done. All of this affirms that Joachim is a holy man in his own right.

It fascinated me to discover that Joachim is presented in just this

---

*See, for example, Exodus 24:18 and 34:28, 1 Kings 19:8, and Matthew 4:2.

way in the Qur'an, as well. The Islamic holy book mentions him several times, referring to him as Imran and saying that his family was honored among the highest-level ancestors of the Israelites. One of the verses reads: "Lo! God preferred Adam and Noah and the Family of Abraham and the Family of Imran above (all His) creatures" (Qur'an 3:33). This indeed puts Joachim on par with nothing less than the founding father of the entire Hebrew faith, which, as we will see, is significant in our story. Muslim spiritual leaders continue to see him as a prophet and apostle to his people to the present day.*

Soon after we hear about Joaquim's inner turmoil and his vow, the Birth of Mary puts the spotlight on his wife, Anne, whom we learn is similarly mourning because she has not yet conceived a child.

WHAT'S IN A NAME?

Let's begin our acquaintance with Anne by first looking at her name. As the philosopher, esotericist, and spiritual adept Rudolf Steiner perceived, "The assigning of names in [religious texts] is conducted on the basis of the person's inner being."[1] We find that Anne's name does indeed reveal a great deal about her character and destiny.

Anne is the French and English rendering of what appears in the Greek versions of this gospel as Anna. In Hebrew, the name is Hannah, which comes from a noun meaning "favor" or "grace." This tells us that the woman who possesses such a name is favored by God or granted a special grace or blessing. Anne indeed is to be blessed with a special spiritual gift, one that has to do with divine conception. This is borne out by the fact that the only other female who bears this name in the Hebrew tradition is similarly granted a divinely born child, as we will see later.

The name Hannah/Anna is also particularly important to our understanding of the events that will unfold because it is remarkably similar to the names of goddesses of the ancient Middle East, where Anne's ancestors and lineage would have dwelled: Inanna, Anat, and

---

*For good references on this point, see Qa'im, 14–15 and Wikipedia's entry on Joachim.

Ḥannaḥanna.* Whether or not these names are linked from a linguistic perspective, I believe they nevertheless point to something significant about the feminine powers that Anne carries, as well as her ultimate divine identity. Let's take a look.

Inanna was a goddess of the ancient civilization of Iraq known as Sumer, which dates back to the fourth millennium BCE. Her name may come from the Sumerian phrase *nin-an-ak,* meaning "Lady of Heaven," and she was the embodiment of a host of powers, including love, beauty, sex, desire, fertility, war, justice, and political might.

The goddess Anat was honored by the neighboring early Semitic peoples of the Levant (modern Syria, Lebanon, Israel, Palestine, and Jordan). Her name may arise from a Semitic root meaning "water spring," and she similarly embodied fertility, hunting, and war.

Ḥannaḥanna was a mother goddess of the Hurrian civilization centered in ancient Turkey in the third millennium BCE, and she was possibly related to Inanna. Her name comes from the Hittite *Ḥanna,* meaning "grandmother."†

We see in all of these associations that by her very name, Anne/Anna/Hannah carries the resonance of the Great Goddess and the Grand Mother/grandmother. This suggests that she holds an elevated sacred role, just like her husband, Joaquim. This is validated in the Qur'an (3:35–36), where, although she is not named, Anne is referred to as the "wife of Imran [Joachim]" and is considered a mystic particularly favored by God.

The similarity between Anne's name and Inanna's is also significant because of this remarkable fact: high priestesses played the role of this Sumerian goddess as part of a sacred marriage rite they would enact for various spiritual purposes.[2] As I am about to show, Anne herself engages in activities that strongly suggest she is carrying out such a ritual, and this is our entry point into the divine-birth mystery revelations of this gospel.

---

*For more see the Wikipedia entries for Inanna, Anat, and Ḥannaḥanna.
†Interestingly, this also calls to mind the Italian word for grandmother, *nonna,* which Sicilian-American feminist cultural historian and professor emerita Lucia Chiavola Birnbaum has pointed out to me.

In the Birth of Mary, this highly blessed Anne is introduced to us at a low point in her life. She is mourning, not only over her childlessness, but also over Joachim's choice to leave on a fast. She declares that she is grieving doubly because she has now become a widow. This affirms what I suggested earlier, that the wilderness vision quest is extremely dangerous, a type of retreat in which the sojourner could actually die. We can imagine that Joaquim is particularly vulnerable to this possibility given that he is elderly.

REVELATION OF ANNE'S ROYALTY

At this point, another person enters the story, Anne's servant Juthine, whose brief involvement offers further information about Anne's true identity. Juthine tells Anne that because the feast day is approaching, a time of celebration, she should rouse herself from her mourning. Her means of cheering Anne up is curious—she gives her a headband that bears a royal insignia, which she says she has acquired from "the mistress of the workshop." While it is unclear who this mistress is, we can guess that she is the leading official of a guild or temple workplace that makes sacred vestments.

To understand the profound meaning of Juthine's gesture, let's bring in the "cheering up" episode of another grieving female, that of the grain goddess Demeter. In Demeter's case, a mysterious woman known as Baubo similarly attempts to make Demeter laugh when the goddess is in mourning after her daughter, Persephone, has been raped by the god Hades. As I show in *Virgin Mother Goddesses of Antiquity*, Demeter's story is filled with divine-birth themes. First, she originally gave birth to Persephone through divine parthenogenesis. Second, Persephone was next in line to conceive a child in this way when her process was interrupted by Hades, who took over her ritual and abducted and raped her. Third, Baubo successfully snapped Demeter out of her grief by lifting her skirt and showing Demeter her vulva, which is hermaphroditic—in other words, it possessed parthenogenetic creative power.[3] With this striking action, Baubo is basically telling Demeter, "You yourself embody both male and female procreative abilities, remember? Lighten up! You're a parthenogenetic queen of creation; what is there to cry about?"

In the Birth of Mary, Juthine is playing the role of Baubo with Anne. The headband she encourages Anne to wear can be seen as nothing less than a royal crown. With this nudge Juthine is reminding Anne of her royalty, her high spiritual status as a priestess of divine birth. She is telling her that there is really nothing for her to grieve over and that she basically just needs to get busy.

Anne irritably rejects her servant's reminder of her sacred parthenogenetic power, however. She is suspicious that Juthine has received the headband from a corrupted person, maybe, as Hock suggests, one of Juthine's lovers.[4] This indicates that Anne as a divine-birth priestess wants nothing in her domain that is associated with common sexuality. Ultimately, however, Juthine's efforts bear fruit. On the heels of this unpleasant exchange, Anne goes into action. She removes her mourning clothes and washes her face. She then does something quite surprising: She puts on a wedding dress.

ANNE'S MYSTERIOUS
SACRED MARRIAGE RITE

I suggest the gospel is revealing a series of ritual actions in which Anne is preparing for a sacred marriage ceremony. We know, first of all, that washing was part of the ritual bath in ancient Sumer. The sacred marriage rite was enacted during the celebration of the new year and possibly on other occasions as well. In the case of the goddess Inanna and the high priestess who embodied her, however, it was the vulva that was washed.[5] So we may ask whether the term "face" in Anne's case is a delicately veiled reference to her vulva by the author of the gospel, or perhaps a word substituted by a later horrified scribe.

What's more, the wedding dress mentioned is the very ritual garment that was worn by the Sumerian priestess who embodied the goddess in a sacred marriage rite.[6] We also see the wedding dress motif in the story of Persephone, who was weaving her wedding dress just before her own parthenogenetic rite when she was interrupted by Hades.[7]

Since we know there is no male partner with Anne now because Joachim is in the wilderness, I believe that the "wedding" she is enacting is an inner one, a sacred marriage with herself. I believe she is entering into the required tantric state for a divine procreative act, like the Muse on the mountain discussed in chapter 2. Again, the earliest divine-birth practice was the kind of parthenogenesis that resulted in the birth of a daughter. Anne is indeed about to conceive a special daughter. So I believe that what we have here is a veiled yet intriguing description of the oldest form of holy parthenogenetic ritual.

The ritual continues as Anne goes to her garden to take a walk. The narrative tells us she does this literally "about the ninth hour" (counting from 6 a.m., according to Hock); that is, about three in the afternoon, a time noted in Acts 3:1 as being designated for prayer. This indicates that Anne is working with sacred timing as a necessary factor in a divine-birth ritual.

Given that many names of divine-birth priestesses and their children contained some form of the word *star,* as mentioned in chapter 2, it may be that the priestesses worked with astrological timing in their rites, and that this is what's being suggested in Anne's particular case. We will see this astrological synchronization dramatically expressed later in the case of Mary's birth of Jesus, where the presence of a star in the sky alerts the great holy men who visit her from the East that a divine child has been born.

The location of Anne's ritual, her garden, is a sacred place, the garden in mystical tradition being a place of magical transformation. The garden metaphor can be traced back to the garden of the gods of the Sumerians* and the Garden of Eden of the Hebrews, realms where humans were thought to be easily in contact with the Divine. Archaeological records show that women were considered the original gardeners, going back thousands of years to the age of the hunter-gatherers,† which means that the garden has always been understood as a domain of woman's magic. Furthermore, in Greece we have the Garden of the Hesperides, which

---

*For more on this, see Kramer, *Sumerians,* 293.
†For some examples of this, see Gero and Conkey, *Engendering Archaeology.*

was a place related to divine birth in particular.[8] The mystical connection between gardens and divine birth can also be seen in a detail in John 20:15, where Mary Magdalene perceives Jesus as a gardener at his tomb after his crucifixion and before he has fully resurrected.

Anne's perching in her special garden under a laurel tree is also significant. In the ancient world at the time when Anne would have lived, the laurel was famously the original centerpiece of the great pilgrimage site known as the Greek Oracle of Delphi, where women served as prophetesses. There, a dramatic legend tells us that the priestess Daphne, who was present during the transition when men took the site away from women, shape-shifted into a laurel tree to escape sexual pursuit by the god Apollo. The tree subsequently bore her name, *daphne;* that is, "laurel." There is plentiful evidence that the priestesses of Delphi were not only oracles, they were also holy women initiated in the practice of divine birth.* We can therefore understand Daphne's story to be the case of a woman who chose to change form (or even perhaps die) rather than have her virgin-birth rite interrupted by a male god. The laurel may have been the signature tree at Delphi specifically because in the ancient world chewing its leaves was a known means of expanding one's consciousness. We know that priestesses used various medicines to achieve the trance state necessary both for delivering prophecy and conceiving children through divine means. Another important piece here is that ancient references to "sleep" and "drowsiness" are signs that a priestess had entered into a trance induced by these powerful medicines for just such purposes.[9] Therefore, we can interpret Anne's "resting" by the laurel tree as a veiled clue that she is entering an altered state of consciousness, presumably by means of chewing its leaves. This places her very clearly in the lineage of divine-birth prophetesses.

At this point, Anne makes a prayer that we can understand to be a ritual invocation to set the stage for what she is about to do. She asks the divine realms for the same blessing that was bestowed on the elder Sarah when she divinely conceived Isaac. In doing so, Anne is verifying that she herself is part of a special lineage of sacred Hebrew women. The

---

*See Rigoglioso, *Cult of Divine Birth,* 180–204, for a review of this evidence.

Qur'an (3:33) confirms this, stating that she is a member of one of two families who are honored in the highest by God, the other being the family of Abraham and Sarah. I will go further to say that Anne is acknowledging the fact that Sarah's birth of Isaac was similarly not a miracle of happenstance, but rather something she had groomed herself to intentionally accomplish. Thus with this prayer, Anne is calling on the divine powers to assist her with a special conception that she will soon accomplish.

IT ALL GOES BACK TO THE HEBREW MATRIARCH SARAH

To understand how Anne is part of a longstanding lineage of divine-birth priestesses, let's explore what we know about Sarah as a holy woman, for she is the first woman in the Hebrew tradition that we know of who had a miraculous conception. There is much more to her story than we have been led to believe, and unpacking her reality and reclaiming her as a divine-birth priestess is extremely important background for the revelations to come about both Anne and Mary.

For this discussion I rely on the remarkable work of Savina Teubal, which I was stunned to discover validated and far expanded on what I intuited about Sarah as I was researching divine birth. In her book *Sarah the Priestess,* Teubal digs deeply into ancient Middle Eastern art, tablets, legal codes, and legends to make the convincing case that this biblical wife of Abraham was nothing less than a female spiritual leader. Teubal identifies her as the first matriarch of Genesis, representative of a culture in which priestesses played the main role.* And as we shall see, there is even more.

What is most intriguing about Teubal's exploration—and relevant to our exploration of the holy women we are looking at—is her argument that Sarah's roles are remarkably similar to those of several types of priestesses in this area of the world roughly around the time she would have lived. These were the *lukur,* the *en,* and the *naditum* (singular,

---

*See Teubal, 71–87 and 106–9, for references supporting my discussion here and in the next few paragraphs.

naditu). Teubal shows that Sarah carried out aspects of all three of these roles at different points in her life. And these roles involved chastity and sacred marriage rites, both aspects of divine-birth practice. Let's take a closer look at how this reveals her to have been a divine-birth priestess, and therefore how her role in Hebrew society relates to what Anne's will be several thousand years later.

First we have the naditum, priestesses of Babylonian society who were unusually independent women of their time. They could do things most other women could not, such as make legal contracts, borrow money, and carry out other business transactions normally denied to women. Usually they were part of the elite, often from royal families. They were allowed to marry despite the fact that they were required to live in a cloister and be celibate in some cases. Even if they were married, however—and this is key to our discussion—the naditu priestess had to remain childless. In the older Sumerian culture, such a priestess would have been called a lukur, and she was a bit more liberated in that she did not live in a cloister, even though she, too, had to remain childless.

Next are the en, essentially high priestesses, usually daughters or sisters of kings. These were women who carried out that remarkable role I alluded to in chapter 2, by embodying specific goddesses in sacred marriage sex rites that they enacted with male gods. At first they conducted their rites without human males, but as things shifted over time, the en enacted these rituals with human kings standing in for the gods.*

We find something strange in the records of old Babylon in the ancient Middle East (c. 1800–1700 BCE): These documents seem to indicate that the sacred marriage rituals were not used to conceive children. Instead, they were used in a magical way to reverse the effects of a natural catastrophe such as drought, to defend the community against raiders, or to ensure the fertility of the land. In fact, as with the

---

*This echoes the changes in the divine-conception practices that I talked about in chapter 2, where the priestess went from engaging in an astral sexual encounter to a human one.

naditum—and this will also be important to our story—at some point laws came about that specifically dictated that the sacred marriage union should *not* result in the birth of a child. If pregnancy occurred, the child would meet a terrible fate: it would be left outdoors in some remote place and exposed to the elements, which usually meant death. Again, I would argue that these shifts represented growing societal control over women and the degeneration of a practice that was originally designed to bring about divinely conceived offspring.

As Teubal shows, we see intriguing signs of these roles, privileges, and restrictions in the story of Sarah. Again, all of this strongly suggests that she was a priestess destined for divine conception. We will see later vestiges of these roles in Anne and Mary. First of all, like the en and the naditum, Sarah was of the elite class among her people. The Hebrew Bible tells us she came from an important family and was not only the partner, but also the sister of Abraham by virtue of the fact that they both had the same father (Gen. 20:12). Teubal has scoured the Bible to uncover hints that Sarah's social status was even higher than Abraham's.

Like the lukur, who were priestesses at a time closer to the period when she would have lived (probably prior to 3000 BCE[10]), Sarah did not have to dwell in a cloister. Instead, Genesis tells us she lived in a tent. Teubal identifies this tent as nothing less than "the abode of the goddess," which served as Sarah's sacred chamber, possibly for a sacred marriage rite. She also says it was what the Hebrew Bible says was a matriarchal storehouse of food for the people.[11] These details accord with the unusually high status of lukur, naditum, and en priestesses, supporting the idea that Sarah incorporated all of these roles. This means she was a high-level holy woman, for sure.

What's more, like certain naditum, Sarah was allowed to marry, but she did not have children, which is also in alignment with the laws regarding both the en and the naditum. Very significant here is Teubal's argument that Sarah's statement, "The Lord has kept me from having children," in Genesis 16:2, is *not a lament about her biological barrenness but rather a reference to the religious laws she had to follow that forbade her from procreating*. Teubal also suggests that Abraham's attempt to sacrifice Isaac, who was divinely born of Sarah, was an effort to obey this law and follow through with the horrific custom of killing any child that was conceived during a sacred marriage ritual. In other words, she was a high priestess with a desire for a child whose womb was restricted and controlled.

Teubal identifies Sarah as an oracular prophetess, as well, and this ticks off another box regarding characteristics of divine-birth priestesses that I talked about in chapter 2. She points to Sarah's visit with Abraham at the oracle-bearing tree at Shechem (Gen. 12:6–7) as a telling clue, for it was there, beneath the boughs of the sacred tree, that the oracle first revealed the larger meaning behind the departure of the two of them from Mesopotamia: Their offspring would inherit the land. Pointing out that priestesses were generally the ones who revealed prophecy at oracle trees, as was the case at Delphi, Teubal suggests that this oracular information was probably delivered by Sarah herself.[12]

Given that the Hebrew Bible tells us that Abraham received prophecy a number of times, I further suggest that Sarah may have been involved in delivering that information in those instances as well. It was at another sacred grove, the Terebinths of Mamre, that Sarah spent most of her life, and Teubal says that Abraham may well have selected this spot because he knew this kind of oracular place would be the perfect home for a prophetess. Teubal also believes that the appearance on this hallowed ground of the divine visitors who gave her the news of her future conception of Isaac was a sign of both the oracular nature of this place and Sarah's importance as a specialized high priestess.[13]

What does all of this tell us? We can see that Sarah was a specialized priestess who was prophetic and meant for celibacy—other than when she was involved in sacred marriage rituals. As we will see shortly, her story suggests that part of her role involved embodying the Goddess and interacting with various male gods or perhaps male priest-kings in sacred sexual rites that were originally meant to bring forth divine children. Taken together, these characteristics tell us that Sarah was nothing less than a divine-birth priestess.

But the details of her story also indicate that Sarah was operating at a time when things were transitioning from woman power to male control. On the one hand, she held the privileges and rites of an older matriarchal society; and on the other, she was restricted by a repressive patriarchal scheme that prevented her from giving birth.

ABRAHAM AS SARAH'S CONSORT, NOT HUSBAND

Here is another stunning possibility that will resonate in the stories of Anne and Mary. If we accept that Sarah was a lukur/en/naditu—that is, a virgin divine-birth priestess—then it may well be that she was never the formal wife of Abraham in the way we traditionally think of that role. Many who are attached to a literal interpretation of the Bible's rendering of marriage as a monogamous sexual relationship between two people will have to take a step back on that one. Yet according to the customs we have looked at so far, as Teubal puts it, "The union of Sarah and Abraham was probably not looked upon as a marriage in which sexual intercourse played a part."[14] Sarah was some form of naditu, and such priestesses had to remain celibate in some cases, remember?

This may explain why Abraham was justified in presenting Sarah as his sister rather than as his wife to two different kings—something that has puzzled most biblical readers. I propose that if they had sex at all, they reserved it for sacred marriage rites only. The rest of the time Abraham would have served as a protector/guardian to Sarah as high priestess. Mark this, because we will see this sexless protector role again with Joachim and Anne, and Joseph and Mary.

Another strange historical artifact confirming that Sarah could have been a specialized priestess with a (mostly, except for ritual occasions) sexless marriage can be found in a document known as the Code of Hammurabi, one of the earliest legal codes, formulated by the Babylonian king Hammurabi (reigned from 1792–1750 BCE). This code of laws strikingly fits Sarah's situation. According to these laws, a married naditu had permission to offer her servant to her husband in order to produce sons. Because the naditum were forbidden to have children themselves, it seems this method was one way in which such women could have their consorts continue a lineage and still adhere to the law that required celibacy.

This law has trouble written all over it, does it not? In fact, the surrogate motherhood arrangement apparently did lead to interpersonal dramas. We know that because the code also specified that if the servant became prideful and uppity as a result of having produced sons in this way, the naditu could demote her to the level of slave—that is, she could treat her anyway she wished, including badly. In Genesis 16 we see this exact situation famously enacted when Sarah hands off the bearing of Abraham's children to her Egyptian "slave" Hagar. After Hagar gives birth to Abraham's son Ishmael, she indeed flaunts her newfound status in Sarah's face. This provokes Sarah's rage. She treats Hagar harshly and eventually banishes her and her son, Ishmael.* Ishmael, in turn, becomes the founding father of the rival faith to Judaism, the Islamic religion.

Although the Code of Hammurabi is dated around 1754 BCE, which is most likely later than the time in which Sarah lived, it points to what may have been a longtime custom by which naditum priestesses could get around controls on their reproduction. I further contend that some naditum in fact continued to practice divine-conception rituals despite whatever laws seemed to forbid it.

Given this, I propose that the surrogate-slave-mother method was not simply a way to allow male consorts to procreate in the face of pregnancy restrictions on their naditum consorts. It may also have been a last-ditch effort on the part of a priestess to having a lineage continue through her partner when she had not fulfilled her mission of having a divine child, despite years of attempts to do so. Clearly this would have been particularly useful in a priestess's elder years, when she was starting to wonder whether she should throw in the towel on her divine-birth practice.

I believe Sarah desperately resorted to the surrogacy arrangement with Hagar when she became worried that she may never give birth to a divine child. Because the fact is, Sarah did not ultimately remain childless; she eventually did have a divine conception. This indicates that she continued to attempt to accomplish this feat her whole life, even into her elder years, despite whatever laws were pressuring her not to.

---

*See Teubal, *Sarah,* 31–41, for an extensive treatment of this topic.

Again, we see many signs that Sarah was operating in a world in transition. It seems priestesses were possibly already feeling the effects of a clampdown on their divine-procreation process even in Sarah's pre-Babylonian time. Nevertheless, I believe she still had one foot in the older female-empowered tradition of sacred marriage in which she had been schooled. Rebelling against restrictive laws, she wanted that divine child, and she wanted it badly.

DETECTING SARAH'S SACRED MARRIAGE RITES

So then, precisely how did Sarah conceive Isaac? Was it through a sacred marriage rite with the Lord God alone? With Abraham as a stand-in? Or with someone else taking on that role? It's important to explore this so that we can compare her situation with what happens later with both Anne and Mary in their divine-conception rites.

Teubal believes Sarah may have engaged in the sacred marriage rite three times in her life. One was with the Egyptian pharaoh (Gen. 12); another was when the three divine messengers prophesied of her coming pregnancy (Gen. 18); and a third was with the polytheistic king Abimelech of Gerar (Gen. 20).[15] Let's take a look at each situation.

The rite with the pharaoh would have taken place when Sarah and Abraham arrived in Egypt. This is the first time that Abraham urged Sarah to say that she was his sister rather than his consort (even though she was likely his naditu wife as well as his half sister). Why? He claimed that if the Egyptians knew he was the consort of such a beautiful woman they would kill him and take her. Perhaps Sarah felt pressured. She persisted in the ruse and was taken to the pharaoh's palace, all the while concealing her real relationship with Abraham. In exchange, the delighted pharaoh offered Abraham a lavish gift of plentiful animals and slaves. Then trouble struck the hapless leader: a plague afflicted his household. With this, the shrewd Egyptian king realized he had been involved in a grave spiritual transgression. He returned Sarah to Abraham and did not even ask for the gifts back.

The second rite may have taken place when divine messengers

appeared at the sacred site of Mamre announcing that Sarah would have a son. We see a hint of a sacred ritual with a divine male presence in the messenger's statement that the "Lord" would arrange for the pregnancy to happen (Gen. 18:11–12).

The third rite would have taken place after this prophecy was made, with Abimelech in Gerar. Once again, Abraham pressured Sarah to tell this king that she was his sister. The biblical text is unclear as to whether Abimelech actually had sex with her, but we hear he was visited by God in a dream and shown that he had done something terribly wrong. As a result, as with the pharaoh, his house was cursed; in this case, all of the women of his household became barren. We can probably safely assume from the severity of the punishment that a sexual encounter between him and Sarah did occur. Abimelech attempted to remedy the situation by lavishing Abraham with livestock and offering the exceedingly generous gift of one thousand pieces of silver.

I believe Teubal rightly proposes that the extravagant gifts these two kings offered in exchange for sex with Sarah are a sign that she engaged in sacred marriage rituals with both. Abimelech's payment of one thousand pieces of silver is a glinting piece of evidence in this regard. Intriguingly, this sum precisely echoes a detail in a sacred marriage ritual depicted in one of the ancient cuneiform tablets of Syria (c. 1300 BCE). In this account, the bridegroom-as-god offers "one thousand shekels" in order to participate with the bride-as-goddess in this special rite.[16] Could the one-thousand figure thus have been a long-standing offering to a sacred marriage priestess in the ancient Middle East? We can similarly interpret the pharaoh's incredibly generous gift of animals and slaves to Abraham as representing the same kind of exchange. In the case of the pharaoh, a sacred marriage rite with Sarah would certainly have been in accord with the documented custom of such royal rites in ancient Egypt. As mentioned in chapter 2, the birth of successor pharaohs was considered to take place solely through rituals of this kind, with the current pharaoh serving as the stand-in for the god, who would enact the divine conception with the high priestess. Thus Sarah as a trained divine-birth priestess was clearly a hot commodity in the ancient world.

The peril that the kings encountered in mating with Sarah is a sign that they were involved in no mere sexual dalliance with an attractive married woman. An important part of sacred marriage rites in ancient Mesopotamia was the correct enactment of the ceremony down to the letter. The proper oracle signs had to be given before such a rite could even proceed. If anything was amiss, or if the priest-king was in any way unworthy or made a blunder in his performance of the long and complicated ritual, trouble could result for him and his people.[17]

The plagues on the houses of both kings indicate that they had violated far more than a traditional marriage covenant. Clearly, by being told that Sarah was merely Abraham's sister, the kings had not been made aware that the two already had a highly sacred covenant together, that of naditu and consort, and therefore engaging with Sarah in a sacred rite was seriously taboo. That the pharaoh did not punish either of them for their misrepresentation and did not ask for his gifts back, and that Abimelech paid Abraham off after the fact, indicates that they were trying to backpedal their errors away.

I propose that if there was any male consort in the rite that led to the birth of Isaac, it was Abraham himself. But even this is not clear. All that Genesis 21:1 tells us about this divine impregnation is that "the Lord visited Sarah as he had said, and the Lord did unto Sarah as he had spoken." It may be that the sacred marriage rite she carried out took place exclusively with God alone or, as we will soon see is most likely the case with Anne and later with Mary, it occurred through parthenogenesis.

MEN'S SACRED ROLE IN ALL OF THIS

It's important to note that there is a fragrance in some of the descriptions of sacred marriage rites or divine-conception rituals that the males may have supported the process spiritually or energetically, rather than physically. I will depart for a moment from my reliance on the documents of antiquity to include the work of the clairvoyant I mentioned in chapter 2, Claire Heartsong. She has received some very interesting information suggesting that men did have an important role in the divine-birth practice. In her book *Anna, Grandmother of Jesus,* Claire identifies the kind of divine pregnancies that Mary's lineage was capable of as "light" conceptions. She says that these conceptions were assisted by a male consort's energy *essence* merging with the priestess's, but not their seed.[18] This makes a good deal of sense to me, and it may be why the male role in the conceptions of Sarah, Anne, and Mary is conveyed in ambiguous terms. It's a mystery that cannot be fully conveyed—and perhaps shouldn't be.

In fact, we see this mystery element explicitly stated by Philo, the Hellenistic Jewish philosopher who lived in Alexandria, Egypt, approximately 20 BCE to 50 CE. After doing this exploration of Sarah I found a fascinating bit in his treatise *De Cherubim*, about the wives of the biblical patriarchs, among them, of course, Sarah.[19] Philo presents the matriarchs as special women—calling them "virtues," in fact—and describes Sarah as the "virtue of princess and guide" in particular. With this he portrays her as the embodiment of womanly royalty and guiding wisdom. In other words, he is telling us what we should be familiar with from all that we have been exploring about her thus far: she is a holy woman, a priestess. Philo specifically states that his interpretation of Sarah, the other matriarchs, and their doings are "secret teachings" (*telete* in Greek) that should not be shared with the uninitiated. I interpret his warning to indicate that his revelations are not just charmingly metaphorical and symbolic, but are referring to actual mystery-school practices that could be understood only by a very few. And what are these mystery practices, precisely?

Philo provides more than clues. He outright affirms that Sarah conceived Isaac first through the "seed" of God. He is then ambiguous as to whether Abraham became involved in this conception. On the one hand he seems to indicate that Sarah "brought forth" her son to Abraham; on the other, he states that it was "unlawful" for Sarah in her role as a virtue/princess/guide to associate with a mortal husband. Again, perhaps he is communicating in a veiled way that Abraham's energy was involved in the impregnation, but not his DNA, for Philo declares that Sarah had a nonsexual relationship with Abraham and that a divine conception did occur.

Notably, he claims that divine conceptions took place not only for Sarah, but also for the other matriarchs: Zippora, the wife of Moses; Rebecca, the wife of Isaac; and Leah, the wife of Jacob.*

We can therefore interpret his term "virtue" to be a title specifically applied to a divine-birth priestess, and we can read his entire passage as a validation of the mystery of divine birth that Sarah engaged in. His writing suggests that all four mothers of Judaism used this process to found the entire Israelite nation—surely a topic for another book. This echoes my finding that children who were divinely born were always seen as significant leaders of their people, either politically, spiritually, or both.

AND THE REAL FATHER IS . . . ?

Whether Sarah's sacred marriage took place with a man as a stand-in for a god, with a disincarnated male deity alone, or through her own self-generated parthenogenesis rite (perhaps energetically supported by Abraham), it resulted in actual pregnancy. According to custom, Abraham was credited with social fatherhood of the child due to his relationship with Sarah. This assignment of fatherhood would have occurred whether he had been involved in the rite or not.[20]

We will see the same situation occurring with both Anne and Mary, where Joachim and Joseph are considered the social fathers of these women's divinely born children, even though they are not their biological fathers. The important point here from the perspective of women's empowerment is that social fatherhood means the males do not claim ownership over the children and their lineage. In this, I believe that Anne and Mary's situations are closer to the original intent of the divine-birth ritual than Sarah's, in which Abraham is given full credit in the Bible for the divinely born son, along with the control that goes with it.

We see Abraham's control operating in how he handles Isaac. Teubal suggests that his attempt to sacrifice the boy may have been another convoluted situation that was meant to appease laws forbidding pregnancies

---

*And in another work (*De Mutatione Nominum*, 132–33), he adds Tamar to the list.

among the en and naditum. Perhaps so. By contrast, my research reveals
that in the original practice of divine birth the ritual sacrificial death
(or even murder) of divinely born children was generally meant to be
done later in their life cycle, after they had become adults and achieved
honor for their divinely inspired leadership. That in the end Isaac was
not slain as a youth confirms that Sarah and Abraham were leaning on
the side of the older matriarchal customs regarding divine birth.

BACK TO ANNE'S CONCEPTION CEREMONY

As we noted, many of the details in Sarah's story are repeated in Anne's,
which links these two women through time as divine-birth priestesses. I
further propose that Anne's ritual at the laurel tree is not the first time
she engaged in an attempt to conceive divinely. No doubt she, like her
ancestor whose miracle she invokes in her prayer, has been schooled in
this art and has been longing for its fruition.

We see a hint of her schooling process later, when she calls in the
temple virgins to give special teachings to her divinely born child, Mary,
and when she completely gives her daughter over to the temple for years
of instruction by these women. Therefore, as with her predecessor Sarah,
in lamenting over her childlessness Anne is not grieving over biological barrenness, but rather over the fact that she has failed to give birth
to a *divinely conceived* child, something she has been trained to do her
whole life.

It's important to take a moment here to observe that in her ritual in
the cultivated garden, Anne is supported by the prayer work of Joachim
in the wilderness. That both of them dive deeply into oracular states
of consciousness may be one of the signs that Joachim supports Anne
on an interdimensional ritual level to facilitate the conception process
energetically, although not physically.

As with Abraham and Sarah, this hints that operating as a kind of
sacred tag team and not engaging sexually may be the very basis of their
relationship—at least for this particular divine conception. Joachim is
likely holding that special role common to all men paired with divine-
birth priestesses: that of economic provider, ritual support person, and

spiritual protector. We see this repeated in the gospel to some degree in the case of Mary, where Joseph provides for her but never actually marries her.

ANNE'S EGO DEATH AS HER PIVOT POINT

As she goes through the steps of her divine-birth ritual, Anne next notices a nest of fertile sparrows in the laurel tree. She now begins to lament that she is lower than even the animals who can freely reproduce all around her in the regular way. I believe this is her dark night of the soul, the point to which even the holiest of people can descend, as Jesus does on the cross when he feels forsaken by the Divine. Such a low point serves as a hell-descent threshold through which a person must cross in order to ascend to the heights. I propose that Anne's version of this is that she has lost hope and faith *not* in her ability to conceive a child through regular means, as some might interpret this passage, but rather in her special capability for divine birth.

Here I would like to call in the story of Anne's biblical namesake, Hannah, the wife of Elkanah, who was similarly in distress over her childlessness and who went to the temple to pray for a son. As with Anne, I propose Hannah's upset was over her failure to conceive a child through divine means, a possibility borne out in the passage about her in 1 Samuel. In that passage the priest of the temple, Eli, thought she was drunk, presumably because of her dramatic weeping. I would say instead that her supposed drunkenness was actually a sign of an altered state of consciousness, perhaps brought about by plant medicine as part of a divine-birth ritual. This idea is supported by the fact that Hannah was no ordinary woman, but rather, as the Bible says, a prophetess, a role that many divine-birth priestesses held. Sure enough, after praying for a son in the temple in her altered state, and after vowing to offer any son that is born to her back to God in service, Hannah did conceive a child: Samuel. Once he was weaned, she made good on her promise and gave him up to the temple.

Like her biblical namesake Hannah, who at her lowest point doubted *her* parthenogenetic powers, Anne is able to pull through.

A divine messenger suddenly appears before her, telling her that her prayers have been answered. The messenger reassures her that she will conceive and give birth, and that her child will be talked about all over the world. Anne has clearly passed the test of ego death after getting to her nadir and rising to the challenge. She succeeds in activating a divine child in her womb. We hear no further details about this process, but we will learn much more about it when we find out how the apocryphal text the Birth of Mary conveys the story of the Blessed Mother's conception of Jesus.

The messenger's announcement emphasizes that Anne is a very high priestess indeed, given that her doings are to become significant for all of humanity. The location of this visitation, by the prophetic tree in the garden, links Anne to her divine-birth priestess ancestor Sarah, whose holy messengers, as we have seen, also prophesied her pregnancy at a sacred tree (Gen. 18:1–10).

ANNE'S SACRIFICIAL VOW

Like Hannah in the Hebrew Bible, Anne vows to offer the child to the Divine as a gift to the temple. Unlike Hannah, however, Anne is a bit more liberal-minded and does not specify that the child need be male. In fact, she makes a point of saying that her vow holds whether the child is male or female.* She also declares that this child will be in spiritual service her whole life—something we will see Mary fulfill, indeed.

The idea of giving a child over to the temple to be raised as a holy person is not something newly introduced in the Birth of Mary; clearly, in the story of the biblical Hannah, we have seen that Hebrew scripture attests to it as a verified cultural practice. This will become important a bit later, when we hear in this gospel more about precisely what such a lifestyle in a temple involved, particularly regarding females.

One implication of this temple service is that Mary will be expected

---

*This is different from what is reported in the Qur'an (3:35–37), where the text implies that Anne expected a male child.

to remain unmarried and celibate for quite some time.* Dedication to the temple suggests that Mary, like her ancestor Sarah, and probably like her mother, Anne, is destined to take on the role of the lukur, naditum, and en priestess in the sense that she will enter the life of a virgin priestess.

JOACHIM, A SHAMANIC PARTNER?

No sooner does Anne offer her child to the Divine than she is visited by two more heavenly messengers. This brings us to a total of three such messengers involved in her conception story in the garden, just as we had with Sarah at Mamre (Gen. 18:2). These two new messengers give her some good news: Joachim is coming back with his flocks, having been told by yet another divine messenger that Anne is pregnant. Presumably he has not had to complete his forty days in the wilderness, as their simultaneous rituals have yielded powerful and swift results. Anne has not become a widow, after all. The two of them have both passed through a dangerous valley of death and despair to soar to amazing new heights in their life together.

The gospel tells us that Joachim gives instructions for the ritual slaughter of animals that will be part of a lavish public celebratory feast. Anne waits for him while standing at "the gate," and as soon as she spots him she rushes to him and passionately throws her arms around his neck.

With these details we are once again in the fascinating territory of the Sumerian sacred marriage rite. A vase dating from the end of the fourth millennium BCE is believed to convey a scene in which the sacred bridegroom (who may, like Joachim, also be a shepherd), bearing abundant gifts of food, meets the high priestess for a ritual at a "gate" that she opens to him. In related images, "gate posts" are identified as the symbol of the goddess Inanna, who is the very deity represented in the sacred marriage ceremony described in ancient Sumerian poetry. As part of the rite, the priestess who embodies Inanna greets

---

*However, this celibacy vow *may* conclude after she divinely conceives a child, for we see in various canonical gospels that Mary is named standing alongside Jesus's brothers and sisters. See Matthew 12:46–47, 13:55–56; Luke 8:20–21; and Mark 6:3. Note that it is not explicitly mentioned in these references that these are *Mary's* children.

her consort with a ceremonial embrace. The couple then prepares by feasting together.*

Is Joachim playing the role of the shepherd who brings food gifts and feasting to the divine-birth priestess with whom he will enact a sacred marriage? As we saw with Sarah, there is ambiguity here, because while these elements contain echoes of the ancient rite, most translators agree that the text indicates that Anne is already pregnant.[21] She herself states as much when she embraces Joaquim. In this, the gospel is conveying information that alerts certain knowledgeable readers to the fact that Anne and Joaquim have together been involved in divine-conception magic. Given the much-emphasized element of Joaquim's absence, I argue that Anne has conceived parthenogenetically, but with assistance from Joaquim's far-off sacred prayer ritual in the wilderness. As Claire Heartsong suggests, perhaps Joachim has lent his essence, though not his seed, to the conception process. After a life dedicated to the practice of divine birth, this couple finally says: Enough! This is our agreement, we need to make this happen, we will do whatever it takes, and this child will be our offering to the Divine in service to the world.

And at long last they succeed.

JOACHIM SEEKS PROOF

We next hear that Joachim wishes to receive some kind of divinely reassuring omen about these events. I believe he wants to know that he and Anne have done everything correctly and that they will therefore not fall into any kind of misfortune the way the pharaoh and Abimelech did in Sarah's story. Joachim decides he will find his sign by looking into the polished disc that is part of the headgear of the priest when he takes an offering to the altar. When Joaquim looks into the disc, "he [sees] no sin in it,"† and we are told that this signifies that any of his violations of

---

*See Teubal, 110–18, for a detailed discussion of these motifs, with references.
†The Greek word in the text is *hamartia*, which is sometimes translated as "sin" but really means "an offense or a violation of the divine law in thought or in act" or "missing the mark."

divine law have been forgiven. I interpret this to mean that he has been given the divine thumbs-up. He is receiving validation that all of the rituals have been done with integrity, and furthermore, that any previous personal or ritual failure on his or Anne's part to bring forth a divine child is now something of the past.

The gospel then fast-forwards to Anne giving birth after nine months, when she asks her midwife whether her child is a boy or a girl. The midwife tells her it is a girl, and Anne touchingly says, "I have been greatly honored this day." This gratitude for a girl child is one of several matriarchal moments in the gospel, showing Anne in contrast to her Hebrew divine-birth forebears, who were legitimized only by the birth of sons. After she finishes her prescribed days of post-birth purification according to Jewish law,* Anne offers her breast to her new infant and gives her the name Mary.

A LOOK BACK AT
ANNE'S MIRACULOUS PRACTICES

The Birth of Mary reveals an intriguing sequence of ritual actions that Anne undertakes as part of her divine-conception rite to bring forth her holy daughter. Let's take stock.

Anne ritually cleanses herself, and this may well include her vulva, for we know this was a common practice for priestesses readying for the sacred marriage ritual. She then dons her "wedding dress," another sign that she is enacting an inner, sacred marriage that will result in conception.

The location of what she is doing is important to the ritual. Working with sacred timing, Anne situates herself in her sacrosanct garden, a place of prophecy. She is assisted in this process possibly by

---

*According to Leviticus (12:5), purification after the birth of a female child requires two weeks plus another "threescore and six days"; that is, a whopping eighty days (almost three months) of refraining from entering the temple or touching anything holy. Presuming that the newly born daughter was considered to be holy, and given that we hear that Anne first offers her breast to the child after her confinement, this may mean that Mary would have been cared for and suckled by midwives and nurses for nearly three months before receiving her mother's touch.

ingesting laurel, which opens her consciousness and allows her to sense the presence of a divine messenger who is assisting her. She uses prayer to call on divine power, and also invokes her divine-birth ancestress Sarah for her help in this rite.

All of this is happening in concord with Joachim's vision quest in the wilderness, where he is most likely calling on divine powers and using his energy to help Anne in her challenging task. When Anne experiences the moment of ego death, that is, the rock-bottom point at which she feels less than even the birds, she achieves the required state of humility, and the conception of her daughter is able to occur. An important part of the process is her willingness to totally surrender this carefully created child to other people and other forces, possibly to rarely see her again.

Before you turn the page, I suggest you take a moment to reflect. How are the revelations about Anne and her ancestor Sarah sitting with you? What does it mean for you to consider that these "miraculous" pregnancies by older women might be more than happy accidents, but rather part of a living women's tradition? Is your reality transforming in any way as you take this material into your awareness . . . and into your body? What implications do you see for our world today . . . and going forward? Again, I encourage you to post your reflections on the Seven Sisters Mystery School Facebook page.

Having traced the epic journey of Anne and Joachim, in the next chapter we will learn more about the early life of the sacred child they name Mary.

CHAPTER 5

Mary's Childhood Training for Divine Conception

The Birth of Mary offers intriguing information that we do not find in the canonical literature about who Mary was and what her life was like before she conceived Jesus. We will now explore what this early Christian record says about Mary's childhood and adolescence.

In this journey together we will uncover signs never before acknowledged—that Mary was a divine-birth priestess-in-training from the day she was born. We'll explore how Anne raised her in a bedroom sanctuary tended by Hebrew temple virgins who began teaching Mary various sacred practices early on. We will then go with Mary to the temple, where she spends the rest of her young life, from age three until early adolescence, and look at what kinds of instruction in divine conception she may have received there.

We will come to understand Mary as a priestess who enjoyed a double empowerment: she came to the planet already an avatar of the Divine Feminine by virtue of her miraculous birth by Anne; and she was given extensive training in order to take up the divine-birth practice on her own. Knowing Mary in this way will help us realize why she was able to conceive a particularly powerful avatar of world service and transformation: her son Jesus.

UNVEILING MARY'S SACRED NAME

As with the name Anne/Anna/Hannah, which linguistically and spiritually connects Anne to significant female ancestors and goddesses, we can assume the name Mary was not arrived at lightly.

In the Birth of Mary, which has survived only in Greek translation, Mary's name is transliterated from the Greek as Maria. The Hebrew version of this name is generally considered to be Miriam (in Arabic and Aramaic, Maryam). Notably, in one place in Mary's gospel her name slips into the text in the Greek version of Maryam, as Mariám.*

Some scholars believe that the name Miriam/Maryam may be related to the verb *mara,* meaning "to be rebellious or disobedient," or to the verb *marar,* meaning "to be bitter or strong." Such meanings certainly suited the first, archetypal Miriam of the Hebrew Bible, the feisty prophetess who helped her brothers Aaron and Moses lead the people out of exile in Egypt. Others, however, believe the name is probably of Egyptian origin, coming from the words *MR* and *MRY* in Middle Egyptian, and that it therefore means something else altogether. These folks have transliterated this word as Meri or Mery, and they generally agree that it is the root of the name Miriam/Maryam, as well as the Greek Maria/Mariám and its anglicized form, Mary.

What is fascinating about this is that Meri/Mery was a sacred title, specifically for the goddess Isis, the Great Mother who gave birth miraculously to her son Horus. Even more interesting is the fact that in Egyptian, Meri/Mery means a host of concepts related to love. In fact, the word translates as "beloved," "desired," "delight," "loving," "lover," and "the loving one." The sacred title Meri/Mery was given to important figures in ancient Egypt, including deities, priests, government officials, and others. A king might be called Mery Isis, for example, which would mean he was the "beloved of the goddess Isis." As it turns out, the concept and practice of love was so important to the Egyptians that they regarded it as the means by which one achieved an exalted state in the afterlife.†

---

*See the Greek in 17:10, in Hock, p. 62, where it appears suddenly as Mariám.
†See Murdoch, *Christ,* 124–137, for an extensive and well-documented discussion of these points.

What we see from all of this is that the name Miriam/Maryam/ Maria/Mariám/Mary means, essentially, "beloved of the Divine," or, stripped down to its essence, "divine love." The name is thus infused with the concept of love that propels one on the evolutionary path, both in this life and afterward. On top of that, the specific divinity the name calls to mind is feminine in nature; namely, Isis. And this was a goddess who well understood divine conception, having conceived her son Horus in her husband Osiris's absence.

These attributes are completely fitting with Mary's identity. She has come to the planet as a high holy being who is deeply connected with the loving spirit of the Divine Feminine by virtue of her own divine birth. And as we will see, she is so connected with the loving feminine spirit that she will be able to co-create another representative of the Divine on Earth through her own womb.

Even more stunning is the fact that scholar and spiritual seer Rudolf Steiner held that Mary was none other than Isis herself, reborn in a transfigured form, and that both Isis and Mary are emanations of Sophia, who is essentially the Great Goddess.[1] The late Indian master Sri Kaleshwar similarly taught that Mary was the most complete human incarnation of the universal divinity he called "Mother Divine" who has ever walked the planet.[2]

In pondering all of this information I have come to the conclusion that, like the term *Mery,* the names Miriam/Maryam/Maria/Mariám/ Mary were not originally personal names, but rather variations of a title, in this case, a priestess title.* As a holy title, it was a triple power moniker that means "Divine Feminine Love," "Feminine Loving One," and "Feminine Beloved"—that is, one who is lover, beloved, and the essence of love all rolled into one.

I contend that this name form was (or became) the marker for an advanced holy woman of a particular type. Such a woman was practiced in the mysteries of the sacred womb and the sacred heart. The Blessed

---

*Miriam may have been a popular personal name among the Hebrews of biblical times precisely because of the power it carried as an honorific. For the popularity of this Hebrew name in antiquity, see Bauckham, *Jesus and the Eyewitnesses,* 89.

Mother was one of these women, but there were others as well. I believe the reason so many holy women of the New Testament held the Hebrew version of this name, including Mary Magdalene, Mary of Clopas, Mary the Mother of James, and Mary Salome, is because they, too, were "Marys"—priestesses of what I call the Holy Order of the Marys.

A GLIMPSE OF MARY'S SACRED SANCTUARY

The Birth of Mary tells us that day by day our infant girl grows stronger, and that when she is six months old Anne puts her on the ground to see if she can stand. Mary does more than stand—she actually walks seven steps back into her mother's arms. Given that most children don't start walking until nine months at the earliest, this is quite a remarkable feat. Anne takes this as an affirmation that Mary is already an advanced being. She scoops her child up and declares that her feet will not touch the ground again until she is given over to the temple.

Anne then decides to turns her bedroom into a sanctuary to properly raise her special daughter. We hear that she forbids anything "profane or unclean" to enter the space. This may also refer to a special purified diet that Anne puts Mary on.[3]

It is clear from this description that Mary's first years are spent in the purity and seclusion of Anne's bedroom shrine. This tells us that Anne is setting her up to be trained as a holy person from infancy. Another account from the Jewish philosopher Philo may shed further light on what she is doing. This is an excerpt from his writings on the Therapeutae, a branch of the Jewish holy order of women and men known as the Essenes, who lived in his vicinity in Alexandria, Egypt:

> [I]n every house there is a sacred shrine which is called the holy place, and the house in which [the Therapeutae] retire by themselves and perform all the mysteries of a holy life, bringing in nothing, neither meat, nor drink, nor anything else which is indispensable towards supplying the necessities of the body, but studying in that place the laws and the sacred oracles of God enunciated by the holy prophets, and hymns, and psalms, and all kinds of other things by

reason of which knowledge and piety are increased and brought to perfection.[4]

Granted, unlike the classical ascetic living situation of the Therapeutae, Anne is in fact feeding her baby in her special room, but we can imagine that her "holy place" is otherwise similar to what Philo is describing here. We can therefore imagine Anne in frequent prayer, contemplation, and sacred song with Mary. In other words, we understand that she is creating the peace, safety, and learning environment that her daughter will need as a foundation for her future life as a holy woman.

The strong possibility that Mary is being given only a purified diet is a further clue that she is being prepared for this kind of life. What exactly is she eating? Whether it's what Jewish law dictates in Leviticus, whether it's the bread-and-water meal of the Therapeutae,* or whether it's something else, we don't quite know. Later, however, we hear that Mary is fed "food from the hand of a heavenly messenger," which may suggest that starting from infancy she ingested sacred medicines that opened her consciousness. It may also suggest that she is able to fast for long periods because the spiritual nourishment she receives overrides the need for much in the way of food.

Anne's choice not to allow Mary's feet to touch the ground reminds me of a religious custom I learned of in Nepal. There, in an ancient Hindu practice still alive today, a young girl is chosen to be a Kumari, a living representative of the Goddess. Once the girl is inducted she is carried in a golden palanquin so that she may not walk on the earth again until the time of her menstruation.[5] I have learned directly from the teachings of the late master Sri Kaleshwar that the reason for keeping a person's body or an object from touching the ground is to prevent any power or energy that has been cultivated in the person or sent into the object from being discharged into the earth. In his tradition, keeping someone or something off the ground can be as simple as making

---

*According to Philo (*De vita contemplativa* 4.37), the Therapeutae were extreme in their dietary pureness, eating only bread and water.

sure that a carpet or cloth is under the person or object so that it never touches either the floor of a dwelling or the physical earth.*

All of this suggests that Anne's seemingly unusual action of keeping Mary off the ground is based on ancient understandings of energy and may well be founded in female-honoring traditions that once thrived on our planet but that have become nearly extinct. It also suggests that Mary was not necessarily restricted from normal movement, but rather that she simply always had some kind of veil, cloth, or carpet between her and the ground beneath her.

ENTER THE HEBREW VIRGINS AS MARY'S TEACHERS

In the Birth of Mary we next hear that Anne does something else quite intriguing: she sends for the "undefiled daughters of the Hebrews" to visit with her own daughter on a regular basis in her shrine room. The phrase "daughters of the Hebrews" is definitely a description used for Jewish sacred women, as we see in the case of the biblical Judith, who is referred to in this way (Judith 10:12). The term *undefiled* (in Greek, *tas amiantous*), most scholars agree, indicates that these women are virgins. So it seems that Anne is calling in consecrated temple virgins to spend time with her daughter.

Hebrew temple virgins? This idea has been met with disdain in certain scholarly circles. Many argue that there was no such thing and dismiss this reference, and with it the entire gospel as a fiction.† Yet with a little digging we do find several possible mentions of temple virgins in Jewish literature, which say that these women were often weavers, a role Mary takes on, as we will see later. We hear of them, for example, in the Mishnah, the first major written collection of the Jewish oral traditions: "The veil of the Temple was a palm-length in width. It was woven

---

*This instruction is part of the Holy Womb Chakra Teachings that Kaleshwar brought forth and that I have also taught, which can be accessed online at SevenSistersMysterySchool.com.

†See, for example, Hock, p. 43 n6:5.

with seventy-two smooth stitches each made of twenty-four threads. The length was of forty cubits and the width of twenty cubits. Eighty-two virgins wove it. Two veils were made each year and three hundred priests were needed to carry it to the pool" (Mishna Shekalim 8, 5–6).

Eighty-two virgins? A garment that ended up being a palm length in thickness? This was a huge project! The enormity of it and the fact that it took place twice a year suggests that these virgins were consecrated; that is, official sacred personnel of the temple complex rather than just ordinary women from the community who periodically rolled up their sleeves for the task.*

We also hear about "weaving virgins" in the Medieval Midrash (homilies) on the festivals of the year known as the Pesikta Rabbati (26, 6). This text tells us that when the Romans sacked Jerusalem in 70 CE, "The virgins who were weaving threw themselves in the flames" so as not to be abducted (meaning, no doubt, raped) by the soldiers. The narrative implies that these virgins indeed lived within the temple complex, along with the priests.

Virgins who presumably lived in the temple and wove the holy veil are also mentioned in the first-century writing known as Apocalypse of Baruch (or 2 Baruch). There we learn again that they had to take action against marauders: "And you, you virgins; who weave fine linen and silk with gold of Ophir, take with haste all (these) things and cast (them) into the fire, that it may bear them to Him who made them, and the flame send them to Him who created them, lest the enemy get possession of them" (2 Baruch 10:19).

We can go back to the Bible itself to find perhaps one of the oldest Hebrew references to female temple weavers. In various translations of 2 Kings 23:7, we hear of special "quarters" in the Jewish temple of Jerusalem where female personnel "wove the veil" of the goddess Asherah—and presumably lived there as well. Given the status of all such women in the previously mentioned accounts, I think it's safe to assume that these

---

*After writing this section, I discovered that the scholar and rabbi Jill Hammer agrees. See her book, coauthored with Taya Shere, *The Hebrew Priestess*, 47–53, for validation of my research here and even further textual evidence from the Hebrew tradition.

women were virgins. That here and in the longer passage in which this mention appears, 2 Kings 23:1–4 (New International Version), we find evidence of goddess veneration, as well as the honoring of the sun, the moon, and the entire starry heavens, means that we are in very early Judaic times. This suggests that the original temple veil may well have been none other than the garment made for the statue of the goddess. In the Greek tradition this task was often the province of virgin priestesses.* The passage in 2 Kings, referenced above, reveals Judaism in heavy transition: King Josiah is violently cleansing the temple of these influences of goddess worship, which were a continuation of practices absorbed from the Canaanite culture. This is a clue that female practices in the temple were undergoing a massive eradication, which may further explain why we hear so little of temple virgins in the Hebrew Bible overall.

The fact of the matter is that religiously oriented virgins were alive and well in the ancient Middle Eastern, Egyptian, and Greco-Roman worlds in which Judaism was born and took shape. Again, going back to the old Babylonian period (c. 1800–1700 BCE) we have the nadi-tum, who were celibate. But more specific to Jewish life and closer to the time of the writing of Mary's gospel we know that various Hebrew women of the late Second Temple period (c. 180 BCE–70 CE) were part of religious movements that required them to adopt an ascetic life-style. In some cases, this meant no sex.

Among these special groups were the Essenes and the related Therapeutae, mentioned earlier. Philo describes the female Therapeutrides as especially devout Jewish women who remained celibate out of their love of God. Intriguingly, he also says they desired "not a mortal but an immortal offspring."† What? Immortal offspring? Although he goes no further with this comment, we are left wondering if it is more than metaphorical. Could it refer to the mysteries of divine conception that he more directly addresses when discussing the Jewish

---

*See my book *The Cult of Divine Birth in Ancient Greece*, 60–61, 70, 135–36, 166–67.
†For celibate women as part of the Jewish order of the Therapeutae, see Philo, *De vita contempletiva* 8.68. For evidence that Jewish women were part of the ascetic Essene community and may in certain cases have been celibate, see Elder, "The Woman Question."

matriarchs, as I noted when we explored Anne and Sarah in the previous chapter? Coming right from the heart of a Hebrew commentator himself, Philo's rascally danglings certainly demand that we not gloss over the idea that virginity and holiness could be paired in the Jewish religious context.

More broadly, throughout the ancient Greek world virginity was an important requirement for many temple priesstesshoods.* And in the overlapping Roman empire we have the famous tradition of the Vestal Virgins, six girls selected between the ages of six and ten who were strictly commanded to remain celibate until they were released from their duties at age thirty. They lived at the temple dedicated to the goddess Vesta and performed important ritual acts that were believed to be critical to the well-being of the Roman state, including keeping the temple flame perpetually lit.

Woe be it to any Vestal suspected of violating her vow of chastity: she would be gagged and veiled, carried on a litter before the public, and forced to descend into a small underground cell whose entry would be barred with earth, leaving her to die alone in the chamber. During the thousand years of the existence of the order, eighteen Vestals were put to death in this manner, with two more who were accused of having sex committing suicide, and two others ending up as paramours of political leaders.[6]

Hebrew virgins . . . The Birth of Mary clearly tells us about their existence, and as we will see later, this gospel suggests that they most likely lived in the temple. Everything we explored thus far supports the idea that such groups of sacred women were a reality, despite scholarly flak to the contrary. In considering this we should keep something else in mind. Over the past few decades, scholars have uncovered a great deal of hidden material about the lives of early Jewish women by applying archaeological finds, inscriptions, and historical texts to the study of the Bible. They have shown, for example, that women may have served as leaders of synagogues in the Greco-Roman world.[7] They have also shown to what extent Israelite women continued to venerate the Divine

---

*Something I discuss throughout *The Cult of Divine Birth in Ancient Greece*.

Feminine in her forms as Asherah and Anat—something nearly erased from the Hebrew Bible under the term "idol worship."[8]

In other words, just because we don't hear a lot about consecrated temple virgins in the Hebrew literature doesn't mean they didn't exist or that they weren't important to temple life.* It may be that even more evidence for them will surface over time as female scholars continue their excavation of the Hebrew past.

The claim is sometimes made that virginity was not important to the Hebrews the way it was to the Christians, and therefore the reference in the Birth of Mary to virgins of the temple is yet more evidence that Mary's gospel is a fictional pastiche of Christian dogma. In fact, virginity had a great deal of religious importance in ancient Jewish life. According to respected Sumerian scholar Samuel Noah Kramer, for rabbis of the first several centuries before Christ, "chastity, virginity, and sexual purity were sacrosanct."[9] Virginity was an important prerequisite for marriage, as we see in the Hebrew Bible. Levitical priests were only to marry virgins (Lev. 21:13). In Judges (21:10–15) we hear of a slaughter that spared "all but the virgins" so that they could be doled out to the victors as wives. A bit later (21:20–23), the passage talks about other virgins engaging in a special dance and then being abducted into forced marriages. Exodus (22:16–17) lays out the law that a man who has sexual relations with a virgin must either marry her or pay the father a dowry if the father refuses to give his daughter over. All of these biblical references show us that virginity was indeed a prized commodity in ancient Hebrew culture.

Furthermore, our friend Philo proposes something rather striking in this regard: that virginity was key to the foundation of Judaism itself.[10] In his discussion of the four Hebrew matriarchs in his treatise *De Cherubim,* he emphasizes the importance of virginity—yes, virginity—

---

*Kateusz, in *Mary and Early Christian Women*, p. 6, states, "Recent research demonstrates that although some of this author's descriptions of Jewish customs [in the Birth of Mary gospel] are not what we might expect given scripture—much like the painted walls of the Dura-Europos synagogue are not what we might expect given scripture—they nonetheless were consistent with Jewish custom as told in the Mishnah and other Jewish texts of that era."

in the ability of these women to divinely conceive children who would be the key leaders of the Israelites. In fact, he writes that Sarah had to engage in inner purifications to return herself to what he refers to as the "class of pure virgins" in order to have a successful sacred union with God to conceive a child. Philo's "class of pure virgins" sounds an awful lot like the "undefiled daughters of the Hebrews" mentioned in the Birth of Mary, doesn't it?

It may be that this aspect of Jewish life is not emphasized in the Hebrew writings, particularly because it belonged to the realm of women, whose ways were being erased in religious life and texts, as we saw with King Josiah. It may also be that the "virginity thing" was, as Philo suggests, part of a secret mystery teaching involving devout women who wanted those immortal offspring mentioned earlier. In other words, it was not discussed openly.

PURIFYING THE BABY MARY

If we embrace the idea that the Birth of Mary is a true account of actual historical events, then it also provides a treasure trove of information about what happens next in Mary's life. We learn that these consecrated temple virgins come around regularly to Anne's bedroom sanctuary to do something special with the young girl. The word in question in some translations is written as *dieplánon,* which means "caused to wander, mislead, deceive." But most would agree that this is not what's taking place here, and therefore it must be a scribal error. Some manuscripts instead assume the word is meant to be *diaplanon,* "to amuse," or *diakonein,* "to serve, to wait on." One scholar has suggested it should be *diaplúnein,* meaning "to wash."[11] Given Mary's pedigree as a divinely born child, and given that she will be sent to the temple to live a specific kind of holy life, I propose that the correct meaning is found in some combination of the above: "to amuse," "to serve," and "to wash." These virgins are priestesses who at times play with their young charge to keep her occupied and delighted, at times serve her, and at times "wash" her; that is, purify her spiritually.

What does this mean? They are most likely applying techniques to help Mary leach out whatever shreds of ego and inner turbulence might be wound into her incarnation as a flesh-and-blood human being. They are probably also imparting to her whatever spiritual instruction or training is appropriate for a divinely born toddler who exhibits a very advanced nature. We can imagine all of this to include special invocations, prayers, songs, dances, energy transfers through touch and thought, and other rites intended basically to raise Mary's level of consciousness, in the same way that Jesus's baptism is understood to have initiated him into a new level of capabilities in his ministry.

The virgins' tending of Mary in such ways would be in alignment with the ancient practices of consecrating and preparing a divinely born child for his or her holy role in life. In my book *Virgin Mother Goddesses of Antiquity* I provide evidence from antiquity for at least three stages of divinization that a divinely born child had to be put through.[12] This may also provide clues as to what the sisters were doing with Mary.

The first stage of divinization was obviously the child's miraculous conception as a result of the mother's parthenogenetic ritual or sacred marriage with a god. The second stage involved a rite enacted sometime between childhood and adulthood to seal the person's divine status. Such rites could involve doing one or more of the following to the child: enclosing it in a chest for a certain period of time, anointing it, exposing it to fire, requiring it to drink a special kind of milk, or immersing it in water.

The third stage of divinization involved the divinely born person's ritual sacrificial death as an adult by being burned in a fire, boiled in a cauldron, struck by lightning, or other means—the main point being that all such rites were intended to confer a magical or divine power on the specially born individual.

I believe the virgins tending Mary had her undergo quite occult-level processes, purifications, and teachings that would allow her to fully seal and embody her divine nature. Perhaps sacred anointing was also part of their work, a process we see when Mary of Bethany, who may well be the Magdalene, anoints Jesus (John 12:1–8). In Mary's case the attending virgins are setting the foundation for her to live a life not only as a holy woman in service to humanity, but specifically as a divine-birth priestess. I contend that Anne herself must have gone through such initiations, just as Sarah and perhaps other Hebrew matriarchs before her. Anne is therefore fully aware of the fact that it is precisely these virgin priestesses who will support her in imparting special knowledge to her daughter; she knows these are not teachings she can give alone.

We see historical evidence for celibate holy women supporting the activities of other, younger divine-birth priestesses in the ancient Greco-Roman world; for example, among the Gerarai, the "venerable priestesses" of Athens. These were fourteen celibate older women who were highly respected in the community and who oversaw religious matters related to the god Dionysus at Athens. They assisted the divine-birth priestess, known as the Basilinna, in her great (and secret) sacred marriage rite with the god.[13] I believe that the Hebrew virgins whom Anne invites into her sanctuary operate in much the same way as the Gerarai, and that with their presence and spiritual gifts they ensure that Mary will be next in line to accomplish a divine birth.

MARY DAZZLES THE COMMUNITY

Mary's gospel tells us that six months after she takes her first steps and begins receiving purifications and teachings from the virgins, Joachim hosts a great banquet to celebrate her first birthday. He invites all the people of Israel, among them the high priests, scholars, and council of elders. That he and Anne can command the attendance of such impressive officials again emphasizes what the Qur'an tells us—that they hold a very high religious status in the community.

When Joachim presents Mary to the priests, they bless her, asking God "to give her a name which will be on the lips of future generations forever." The high priests then ask God to "bless her with the ultimate blessing, which cannot be surpassed." With this, I believe the highest Jewish religious personnel are honoring Mary as nothing less than the most advanced holy person on the planet, one whose gifts will not be superseded by any other human being.

What is happening here is that the priests are prophesizing about her future role. The late Hindu saint Sri Kaleshwar, who has discussed how and why it is that Mary was the most advanced holy person who ever lived, presents her as a high-level adept who possessed even greater power than her son Jesus and explains that she served as his first, primary, and ongoing teacher.[14] This stunning revelation, I believe, marks the culmination of the gospel's vision of "Mary the unsurpassed" as one that is only being fulfilled today, at this time of greatest need on the planet for a Divine Female master.

When Anne returns to her sanctuary with Mary after the blessing, she is apparently intensely inspired by this enormous prophetic blessing, because we hear that she next composes a song to God. This reminds us of the practices of the Therapeutae, who were also known to "compose psalms and hymns to God in every kind of meter and melody imaginable."[15] Anne's song praises God before the twelve tribes of Israel for having given her this child. Looking at this in the traditional patriarchal way, we might see this as the gospel giving (a male) God all the credit rather than Anne. But there is something in the text that subtly turns this around. Anne describes herself in this song as "single yet manifold before [God],"* a phrase that scholars tend to find puzzling. When we understand that Anne has been a virgin priestess of divine birth herself, its meaning becomes clear. She has been the "single" or solo woman; that is, the parthenogenetic woman, the sole weaver at the loom. Yet from that holy single state she has become manifold; that is, more than one. Not only has she given birth to a divine child, her divine lineage will continue through Mary's birthing of Jesus, and his spreading of spiritual teachings to the multitudes. In other words, Anne is honoring her own accomplishment, too.

OFFERING MARY TO THE TEMPLE

When Mary turns two, Joachim feels the nudge to make good on their promise to dedicate their daughter to the temple. Anne hesitates, showing herself to be a caring mother who is concerned as much for her daughter's emotional well-being as she is for her sacred oath and her

---

*The Greek reads *monooúsion poluplásion enopion autou.*

child's divine destiny. She convinces him to wait another year so that Mary won't miss them as much.

A year later, then, it comes time. Joachim calls for the virgin priestesses—and I assume these are the same ones who have been purifying and serving Mary in the bedroom sanctuary. He has each of them take a lamp, light it, and carry it with them as they escort Mary out of the house to the temple. The idea is that the lamps will create a haze of light around Mary so that if she turns around she won't be able to see her parents, who are trailing behind the holy retinue. We can assume, then, that this sacred procession is taking place at night.

At the temple, the priest welcomes Mary, kisses her, and blesses her. He then proclaims that God has exalted her name among all generations and that it is through her that the people of Israel will find redemption "during the last days." With this, we see that she is being honored once again as the most holy person of all times, bar none, for she is being given the redemptive role later assigned to Jesus. The priest further honors Mary by setting her down on the third step of the altar, an area normally reserved for the most important holy personnel. This is a sign that she is being inducted as a high priestess of the temple.

At this point, the young avatar does something remarkable: she not only takes her first consecrated steps, she dances. This reminds us of the reference to the dancing virgins in Judges 21:20–23, and also the account in Exodus 15:20 of Miriam, sister of Aaron (and Moses), taking up the timbrel and dancing. I propose that the child Mary is enacting a ritual dance. Given that she has spent the first three years of her life with no exposure to the outside world, I would expect that this dance is something the virgin priestesses have taught her. Among the many teachings and blessings they imparted to Mary, we can assume that they've taught her precisely how to behave in a temple setting. In the next chapter we will see Mary's dancing referred to in a way that connects it with the "songs of the divine messengers" that she is privy to while living in the temple. So Mary's dancing is the first revelation to the public that the teachings she has received to train her as a high-level priestess have stuck.

By demonstrating such adeptness with the important rite of sacred dance at such a young age, Mary impresses everyone present in the temple and immediately becomes a beloved figure in her community. She also displays exceptional maturity by not looking back at her parents, something at which both of them marvel. These actions affirm that Mary, like a young Dalai Lama, is well beyond her years, already manifesting the advanced traits of a holy person. The priest's action of taking her close to the sacred altar tell us that she is now an official virgin priestess of the temple. With this, Anne and Joachim say a silent goodbye in their hearts to their beloved daughter and turn back home without another word.

THE WORLD OF TEMPLE VIRGINS— BABY BEARS AND VESTALS

Based on the evidence we looked at earlier for the existence of temple virgins, we can assume that there was indeed a role for girls who were consecrated to the Hebrew temple—just as we saw there was for the son of the biblical Hannah, who was similarly given away to become a servant of God. This means that for the education of one such as Mary there must be female personnel to instruct her. I propose that the virgins who have been training her at her home and who have accompanied her to the temple continue to serve as that teaching entourage, but now their work takes place in this officially sanctified setting. It is here in the temple where Mary learns more fully how to become a divine-birth priestess herself. But before I discuss that, I want to first provide some broader cultural context.

The idea of the temple training of young virgin girls, where we find the fragrance of divine birth lingering, is not foreign to the ancient world. We see it in Greece, for example, where girls aged five to ten, known as the Arktoi, were taken in for training in a dance ritual that honored the virgin mother goddess Artemis. They were required to wear saffron-colored robes as a sign of their role, and they had to live in seclusion for up to a year in special temple buildings known as parthenons—a word, as I have shown, that refers to the goddess Artemis as both virgin (parthénos) and mother. Their dance involved their "becoming the bear"; that is, becoming Artemis,* which I believe means they were specifically connecting with Artemis's parthenogenetic ability.[16] In other words, here we have an example of training, dance, and virgin-birth themes all related to the special holy induction of young girls.

In ancient Rome we have the Vestal Virgins, girls who were handed over by their parents in childhood to live near the temple of Vesta, goddess of the hearth. Perpetually dressed in white garments, they spent their first decade learning their functions, their second performing them, and their third instructing the younger ones. In addition to anxiously ensuring that the temple fire stayed perpetually lit, they participated in a demanding schedule of rites throughout the Roman religious calendar, including elaborate rituals connected with fertility and the agricultural festivals of planting and harvesting.[17] Like the naditum, they enjoyed various legal, business, and social rights that were otherwise denied to common women.[18]

Where we blatantly see the Vestals' connection with divine birth is first in the nature of the goddess they served, Vesta. The Roman form of the Greek goddess Hestia, Vesta was the goddess of the hearth and the fire element, which was thought to be equated with virginity because it "consumed" but did not "produce." At the same time, however, Vesta the virgin represented the Earth and was considered the center of the universe.[19] In other words, she was also a generative force. So in Vesta we once again have a being who is a Virgin Mother. The Vestals embodied that very same duality. While they were virgins, they were also in charge of life-giving fire and fertility rituals.†

We next see the divine-birth theme in association with the Vestals in the story of the first-named Roman Vestal, Rhea Silvia. According to Roman historian Titus Livius (Livy 1.4.2), Rhea Silvia conceived Romulus and Remus, the founders of Rome, by the god Mars. This

---

*The name Artemis, referring to the goddess of the hunt and wild animals, is related to the Greek _árktos,_ or "bear." The goddess had a bear cult in locations on the Attic peninsula.

†See Lindner, 1, for a brief analysis of Vesta's and the Vestals' duality in this regard.

would fall into the category of sacred marriage with male gods, discussed in chapter 2, as being a stage of the divine-birth practice. In short, this is telling us that divine-conception practices were at the very foundation of the order of the Vestals.

We see other hints that the Vestals were associated with divine birth, clues that poke through history in distorted ways in various literary fragments. I was struck to learn that when the chief high priest of the College of Pontiffs of ancient Rome, the pontifex maximus, initiated a new girl into the order, he used a ritual phrase in which he called her *amata,* "beloved one."[20] This is a strange term of endearment for a girl who would give up all pleasures of love and live in chastity as the texts convey to us—unless we consider all that we've learned about divine birth so far. Amata recalls Mary's name, which itself is a form of "beloved" and, in its Egyptian form, a reference to the goddess Isis, who is associated with divine birth. Under this word, then, is an implication that a Vestal was a "chosen one," a girl chosen for some kind of love union with the Divine. This makes me ask: What was the real relationship between these sacred initiates and the pontifex maximus, who had full control over them to the point where he could punish any of them for offenses through flagellation, sometimes, as the ancient texts tell us, in dark places where they lay naked under the cover of a veil?[21]

My ears also perked up at something the writer Plutarch says: that some people believed the Vestals performed "certain secret rites" (Numa 9:8).[22] These priestesses also shared the care of the holy relics and sacred objects with the Salii, priests of none other than the god Mars.[23] What were these secret rites, and what was the real relationship between the Vestals and the priests of a god who had impregnated their lineage founder? Why did it take a full ten years for these girls to learn what they needed to know in order to carry out their duties? As we will see, this is about the same length of time that Mary will need to learn how to conceive divinely. Is there a relationship here, and were the Vestals learning something far more secret than we have been led to believe?

We need look no further than two public incidents in the Roman record to find outright evidence that the Vestals were indeed used by the emperors in occult divine-birth rites. The controversial and flamboyant Roman emperor Elagabalus (or Heliogabalus, c. 202–222), who was a high priest of the Syrian sun god, married the Vestal Virgin Aquilia Severa not once but twice, the second time after an intervening marriage. Aquilia was the daughter of an official who served under the Roman emperor Caracalla. According to the Roman historian Cassius Dio (*Roman History*, 80.9), Elagabalus tied the knot with her, claiming the marriage would produce "godlike children." Good heavens, there we have it, in black and white!

Similarly, another wild card emperor, Nero, also seduced a Vestal.[24] And neither she nor Aquilia were punished in the customary way for having violated their vows. I surmise that these rogue emperors, through their own flagrant disregard for tradition—and for the discretion that tradition required—simply made public what was already going on beneath the surface with the entire Vestal Virgin order. They were certainly not going to have their consorts punished for carrying out this long-standing secret, sacred role.

A final word on the use of the Vestals' wombs, and this relates to their tending the fire element. Plutarch (Camillus 20.3–4) says King Numa believed fire was nothing less than the eternal power that preserves and actuates the universe—in other words, the smoldering kundalini/womb fire of the Great Goddess. In tending that fire as virgins, I believe the Vestals sacrificed their own womb power to a larger force. Unfortunately, that force was the entire Roman machine itself. Given that the Vestals would be beaten if they ever let the flame die out, their role became one of enslavement.[25] This bondage, and the secret use of their wombs in probable occult rites, represented the full co-opting of their kundalini powers of divine generativity by a degenerate Western patriarchy. As we will see, Mary, in contrast, is able to appropriately harness her kundalini fire/womb power in service to actual pregnancy.

All of this is to say that the temple training of females with divine-birth associations was not unusual in the ancient world before and around the time of the events depicted in the Birth of Mary.

LIKE A DOVE, SHE EATS

If we carefully turn over the brief description the gospel offers of Mary's tenure in the temple, we can uncover quite compelling evidence that she receives special training there. The narrative tells us two things only: that she lives in the temple, and that during her years there she is "fed there like a dove, receiving her food from the hand of a heavenly messenger." This is succinct, but packed with coded information, so let's take a look.

The text essentially equates Mary with the dove. This is significant given that in antiquity this bird was associated with divine wisdom, divine will, and a person's eternal soul. Roman symbolism, for example, depicted the human soul as a dove held in the hand of the person who has died, or as a dove flying out of the mouths of dead Roman emperors. In Egyptian tomb paintings, a dove sometimes hovers above the dead person as an image of the soul that is about to go back to its eternal home in the stars.[26] In fact, the dove was perceived not just as the soul of a human being, but as the essence of divinity itself, often in its feminine aspect. The dove is the symbol of many ancient goddesses, including Ishtar and Ashtoreth, important goddesses in the ancient Near East and rival deities to the male god of the Hebrews during the early period of Judaism.

So in this one small word, *dove,* the author of this gospel is telegraphing a great deal about the original nature of Mary as a special embodiment of the Divine Feminine. But there is more: it tells us about her spiritual development as a soul who is in her own ascension process, as well as a priestess who has a mission to accomplish on Earth, because the dove also has a strong association with virgin birth. We see this connection in an ancient story where the goddess Aphrodite is born out of a great egg fallen from heaven that doves sit on to hatch—which is to say she is born parthenogenetically, and the doves are the agents of that birth. In addition, the dove's ability to occasionally lay barren eggs without having sexual intercourse, creating what the Greeks called a "wind egg," may have enhanced its reputation as a symbol of virgin birth.[27]

More to the point, equating Mary with the dove, I believe, tells us specifically that she was continuing to receive training in divine-birth practices while in the temple, for the dove was a significant symbol of prophetic divine-birth priestesses. For example, at the ancient oracle of Dodona in Greece, priestesses who both gave prophecy and conceived divine children were called "doves."* The term for "doves" in Greek, *peleiades,* also connects them with the Seven Sisters of the Pleiades, important stars to the ancient Greeks. These Pleiadian sisters were considered virgin mothers of much of the human race and were also seen as "doves."[28] The dove symbol therefore not only points to Mary's own parthenogenetic ability, it also suggests that she, too, may have been working with the ancient starry ancestors known as the Pleiades in her divine-conception practices.

So the gospel's statement that during her time at the temple Mary "fed there like a dove, receiving her food from the hand of a heavenly messenger" implies that the means of preparing her for her role as a "dove," that is, a divine-birth priestess, involves (1) special food, and (2) heavenly messages or teachings. On the most practical level, this may mean that just as she did in her mother's shrine room, while in the temple she continues to receive some kind of energetically purifying diet.

But the reference to the "heavenly messenger" indicates this "food" may have been some kind of sacred herbs or medicines that allowed her to continue to open her consciousness to the heavenly realms and even raise the nature of her entire soul essence. All of this may be needed for her to enact a divine-birth ritual—just as her mother, Anne, may have needed laurel as part of her own divine-conception rite. We see support for this idea in the ancient Greek notion of ambrosia, a substance that could confer divinity and reinforce immortality, even on the gods. Notably, it was doves who fed ambrosia to the god Zeus to tune him up to divine status![29]

Whether Mary imbibed special medicines or not, receiving food

---

*Along these lines, the Rosicrucians, who claimed to be inheritors of the Greek esoteric tradition, considered the Colombe, "the dove," to be a symbol for conscience, and they perceived her as a Vestal Virgin who was a prophetic priestess. See my book *The Cult of Divine Birth in Ancient Greece,* 151.

from heavenly messengers can also mean that she is in some kind of regular contemplative communication with the angelic realms, and it may also refer to the high-level teachings and empowerments that she receives from these intelligences. These teachings and empowerments may literally serve as a kind of nourishment that feeds her body, lessening her need for actual food.

The reference, then, to Mary's association with the dove and with heavenly food in this brief history of her temple life indicates that the special empowerments she receives to enhance her own divine nature and her divine-conception abilities have stepped up considerably since she was in her mother's sanctuary. I believe Anne knew this would be the case if she wanted her daughter to continue in her lineage, and that this is the real reason she had to hand her precious daughter over to the temple.

WILL MARY BLEED?

The gospel fast-forwards to when Mary turns twelve, just around the age a girl typically starts menstruating. The priests are in a quandary, apparently because according to Jewish law (Leviticus 15:19–33), once she begins her monthly flow she will render the temple "unclean." They meet to contemplate what to do about this.

At face value, the Hebrew perspective that menstrual blood is polluting seems patriarchal, and it may well be.* Do we not assume that the time of menstruation is the time when women step into their greatest female reproductive power? Ejecting them from a sacred sanctuary at this threshold point seems like something intended to throw women off rather than support them in their holy conception ministry. Furthermore, would we not assume that if Mary is being trained in divine birth, the accomplishment of it would need to take place in

---

*However, various Native American cultures also restrict menstruating women from participating in sacred rituals, but from a completely different perspective. They consider women's menstrual blood to be so powerful that it could lead to disruptions in the ceremonies. Thus the sequestering of menstruating women is considered an honoring of women's power. The sense is different in the Hebrew tradition.

the sacred precincts where the virgin priestesses continue to dwell?

The gospel as it has been preserved and handed down to us indicates that the culture is in transition about these issues. The events it depicts occur at a time when patriarchy is continuing to encroach on women's sacred power. Clearly, even the priests are confused about Mary's elevated status, because they do not categorically eject her from the temple. Rather, they suggest that the high priest enter the Holy of Holies and pray about the matter to receive divine guidance as to what exactly to do.

Another question I wish to raise here is whether the priests may be jumping the gun, so to speak. In chapter 2 I discussed the possibility that women who conceived children divinely did not actually have a menstrual flow due to their eating a special vegetarian diet, combined with practicing celibacy. We have seen that Mary may have been fed a special diet, and I will discuss this further in what follows.

Is she perhaps not destined to menstruate, after all, and has that fact been hidden from the male priests by the virgins who have been keeping the specific processes of divine birth veiled as a sacred mystery, as Philo instructs in his writings? Does the cessation of menstruation as a requirement for divine conception help explain why postmenopausal priestesses like Sarah and Anne were able to miraculously conceive children—in other words, because the menstruation cycle was never needed to begin with? Does this also explain how the virgins who taught Mary and who may have been a range of ages presumably remained in residence at the temple without a problem? Maybe they're not menstruating either . . .

I would also ask whether this event represents yet another instance where the gospel was tampered with by later scribes. As it turns out, religion scholar George Zervos convincingly makes this argument. By scrupulously analyzing the oldest surviving manuscript of the Birth of Mary, Zervos has concluded that its original layer depicts Mary's encountering the divine messenger who will later announce her pregnancy *while she is still in the temple*. This contrasts with later editions of the manuscript, which state that the announcement of her pregnancy takes place in the house of Joseph after she has been asked to leave the temple.[30] That the announcement did take place in the temple is echoed in another piece of New Testament Apocrypha, the Gospel of Bartholomew, which may have been written as early as the second century.[31] Bartholomew 2:15, suggests that Mary's conception rite does indeed take place in the holy precinct where she has been trained.

DIVINING MARY'S GUARDIAN

Whether Mary conceives inside or outside the temple, I will proceed with an exploration of the events as depicted in Hock's version of the gospel, because it provides such rich information about Mary, the people around her, and the circumstances that take place.

At this point, the story gives us the name of the previously anonymous high priest of the temple, the man who has honored, received, and blessed Mary in all of her temple appearances. This is Zechariah. He will prove to be a key character in the story as the consort of another female elder who will divinely conceive a child; namely, Elizabeth, a blood relative of Mary and the mother of John the Baptist.

To decide Mary's fate, Zechariah enters the Holy of Holies, the innermost sanctuary of the temple where the Divine Presence resides. Here he begins to pray. Given that the Holy of Holies was entered only once a year by the high priest on the Jewish Day of Atonement (Exodus 30:10), that he is entering the chamber to consult on the question of Mary confirms her importance and high status. It also confirms what was the case with all Hebrew high priests of the old order: that Zechariah is a prophetic holy man who is able to receive divine oracles directly.

While in prayer, a spirit messenger tells him how to get out of his dilemma. He is instructed to gather all the widowers among the people and have them each bring a staff. The messenger says that Mary is to become the *guné* of the one to whom a sign is given. This Greek word can mean "wife," although a more accurate translation is "woman." As we will see, in this gospel Mary never actually marries the man who is chosen, Joseph; instead she becomes his ward.

Zechariah goes to work. He sends out heralds to the surrounding territories of Judea. They sound the trumpet of the Lord (perhaps the shofar) to call the widowers together, who come with their staffs in hand. Among them is Joseph the carpenter, who reluctantly joins the crowd despite the fact that he's in the middle of work. The widowers hand over their staffs to Zechariah, who enters the temple to pray again. When he finishes his prayer, he takes the staffs outside and hands them back to each man. The last man to receive his staff is Joseph. At this point the expected sign is revealed: to the surprise of everyone present, a dove emerges out of Joseph's staff and perches on his head. Here again is another reference to the dove as a sacred totem strongly and appropriately connected with Mary and divine birth. Zechariah proclaims that Joseph is the divinely chosen man to take Mary under his care and protection.

Let's be clear: Zechariah does not specify that Joseph should *marry* Mary, and in contrast to what appears in Matthew and Luke, nowhere in Mary's gospel does a marriage ever take place between them. Moreover, the high priest specifically characterizes Mary as a "virgin of the Lord"—essentially a virgin priestess, which marks the first time in the gospel we hear about her status in this regard. The timing of this event is significant because it emphasizes her holy role as a divine-birth priestess, as well as Joseph's divinely ordained status as her guardian. This is the same arrangement that took place between other virgins and their companions, including Sarah and Abraham, and Anne and Joachim. The events leading to Joseph's assignment give us further information about this process; namely, that such arrangements were generally determined through rituals and signs.

Despite the hand of the Divine in the matter, Joseph is apparently not too keen on the undertaking. He objects that he already has sons and that he is an old man.* Given Mary's youth, he fears he will become the butt of jokes among the people of Israel. This implies that although he is not being asked to marry her, there is a sense that his relationship with her will be publicly perceived as a kind of marriage arrangement.

---

*Again, one of his sons may be the James who claims authorship of Mary's gospel.

I propose this is why Joseph and his predecessors Abraham and Joachim are presented in the texts as "husbands"—they are in a kind of intermediary relationship with their priestess-consorts that is neither conjugal nor strictly paternal or brotherly. We will see something similar with Zechariah and his "wife," Elizabeth.

Zechariah will have nothing of Joseph's resistance. He admonishes him to remember the negative fate of others who have defied the will of God and pressures him to take Mary with him. Joseph reluctantly complies and takes her into his home. However, after settling her in, he announces that he is leaving for an unspecified time to build houses, telling her that he is putting her in the Lord's care. This is the last of Joseph that we will hear of for a while.

ALL RIGHT . . . NOW, EXACTLY *HOW* HAS MARY BEEN TRAINED?

Reviewing the training that Mary receives to prepare her to conceive Jesus miraculously, let's recall that the process starts with the selection of her special name. Her mother, Anne, establishes Mary's special energy by gifting her with the sacred moniker that means "Divine Love."

Then Mary is sequestered from the rest of the world in Anne's special sanctuary, where her feet are not to touch the ground until she makes her way to the temple at age three. She is fed a special diet, which may include sacred medicines to open her consciousness, and her regimen may also involve fasting. She is protected from impure influences of any kind, which allows her to keep her emotions calm and her thoughts elevated. This may well purify her body to the point that she does not need to menstruate when puberty hits.

Mary is tended by virgin priestesses of the temple, who take her through a series of further purifications. These no doubt involve physical cleansing as well as inner cleansing. Activities such as prayer, song, mantra recitation, and other rites not revealed by the gospel may be part of her inner work. These virgin priestesses most likely teach Mary how to work with the sacred sounds of the angelic realms, which we will hear more of later, and they also teach her sacred dances.

When she is three, the virgins take Mary to live in the temple. There her training continues with the help of special foods and sacred medicine so she can continue to expand her consciousness and prepare to be a "dove"; that is, a priestess of miraculous conception. Eventually she is divinely assigned a sacred male guardian, Joseph, whose role is to look after her and support her for her coming work.

At this point, with Joseph's departure, we have a similar scenario as that of Anne and Joachim, where there is an extended separation between the two partners. It is during this time apart from her male guardian that Mary will conceive Jesus.

This is once again a good place to invite your personal musings. What are your impressions and feelings as you absorb this information about Mary's upbringing? How is any image you may have had about Mary transforming for you as a result of this new information? Where does it land in your heart, mind, spirit, or body to consider the possibility that she was purified, blessed, and taught in very special ways for her very special role from the time she was six months old? What do you think this information might mean for the women of our world who wish to go deeper into their own spiritual practices? Have you had any response to the pioneering information presented on the Vestal Virgins as being divine-birth priestesses? Please share your views on the Seven Sisters Mystery School Facebook page.

CHAPTER 6

Mary's Divine Conception of Jesus

The Birth of Mary gospel tells us about Mary's sacred conception of Jesus in far greater detail than we find in the gospels of Matthew and Luke. Such details, when explored from the perspective of the research on divine birth that we are considering throughout this book, reveal a remarkable story about how Mary was able to accomplish the unusual conception for which I believe she was trained.

We are about to take a foray through the many clues and symbols found in Mary's gospel that provide occult information about the nature of her divine conception ritual. We will explore how Mary's role as a "weaver" is the first sign that her real work is devoted to conceiving a divine child, and we will uncover evidence that she uses technologies such as sacred sound in this process. We will also consider the possibility that she is supported in her divine conception by a group of priestesses both young and older that includes her relative Elizabeth, who miraculously conceives John the Baptist close to the time when Mary conceives Jesus. What will come to light for us is a vision of Mary as part of a sisterhood of holy women of virgin birth across time and space.

THE "WEAVING" OF THE SACRED CHILD

Mary's gospel tells us that after she is living alone in Joseph's house for a time, a council of priests decides that it's time to "make a veil" for the temple. For this task, the high priest Zechariah instructs temple assistants to leave and search everywhere to locate the "true virgins from the tribe of David."* These assistants scour the land to find seven such women, and they call them to the temple. Zechariah then recalls that Mary, too, was from the "tribe" of David and was also considered pure in God's eyes. The temple assistants find her and bring her to the temple as well.

As we saw in chapter 5, there was at the time of this gospel's writing a custom of having virgin weavers construct the temple veil. This was a big, important job, especially given that the veil was quite large and heavy. The Birth of Mary tells us that the virgins required for this particular veil are not in the temple but are scattered far and wide, such that they must be gathered together. This detail may be a rewriting of the original, where Mary and possibly these other virgins are still living in the temple. Whatever the case, it is clear that the virgins needed for this particular task must be from the "tribe" of David, and they must be pure; that is, dedicated celibate women.

Now we know that among the twelve tribes of Israel there is no such "tribe" of David,† so the text must be referring to the House of David; that is, the lineage of King David as laid out in the Hebrew Bible. In Matthew 1:16, Mary is listed as being from David's house, but only by virtue of her relationship with Joseph, who is apparently from this lineage.‡ Mary's gospel, however, bumps Mary up a notch by explicitly indicating that she is indeed, by blood, a member of this important royal house from which various kings claimed their right to rule over the Israelites. It seems that a specific royal bloodline is being called on here, one connected to one of the most important Israelite leaders. This is our first clue that the weaving project Mary is involved in has to do with far more than just creating a temple textile.

At this point, the seven virgins, plus Mary, are taken into the temple. The number seven that is emphasized is significant, especially

---

*The original Greek is *tas parthénous tas amiántous*.
†David comes from the tribe of Judah (Matthew 1:2–6).
‡Luke (1:5, 36), in contrast, allies Mary more closely to the lineage of Aaron by virtue of her being a relative of Elizabeth.

because it is a far lower number than the eighty-two virgins involved in such weavings that we saw referenced in the Mishnah. That this is such a small, intimate group, in contrast to the number of personnel normally needed to carry out a huge project of this nature, is another clue that something else is going on here.

In addition, with the sacred number seven I again bring our attention to the Seven Sisters of the Pleiades, considered by the ancient Greeks and many other traditions to be the seven virgin mothers of the world. I am also reminded of the fourteen Gerarai of Greece who assisted the Basilinna, the divine-birth priestess, in conducting her sacred marriage ritual with Dionysus. In that case we have seven times two, plus the priestess herself. Later I will discuss the significance of the number eight to this process, which is the total number of women involved when Mary is included.

Let's take a moment now to look at what the temple veil is all about. In the Jewish tradition, the veil marks off the Holy of Holies, the inner sanctuary of the temple, which is defined by four pillars. This is the most sacred chamber of the temple, the place where the Divine is considered to dwell. It is also where the Ark of the Covenant, which contains the Ten Commandments of Moses, is placed. In his description of the veil in the First Temple in ancient Jerusalem, the first-century Jewish historian Josephus gives us an extraordinary picture of what such a textile may have looked like:

[B]efore these doors there was a veil of equal largeness with the doors. It was a Babylonian curtain, embroidered with blue, and fine linen, and scarlet, and purple, and of a contexture that was truly wonderful. Nor was this mixture of colors without its mystical interpretation, but was a kind of image of the universe; for by the scarlet there seemed to be enigmatically signified fire, by the fine flax the earth, by the blue the air, and by the purple the sea; two of them having their colors the foundation of this resemblance; but the fine flax and the purple have their own origin for that foundation, the earth producing the one, and the sea the other. This curtain had also embroidered upon it all that was mystical in the heavens, excepting that of the [twelve] signs, representing living creatures.*

From this description we see that in the premier temple of Judaism the veil was particularly ornate and covered with symbolism representing the four elements (earth, air, fire, water), earthly creatures, and the starry heavens. In short, it represented an image of the universe itself.

So Mary and the virgins are to weave the universe. In light of this, what the Birth of Mary next tells us is noteworthy. We hear that the high priest Zechariah calls for the divinatory method known as the "casting of lots" to help him decide which virgins will take which threads to be woven or embroidered onto the veil.† Zechariah specifically mentions seven thread colors that will be assigned to the virgins, some of which echo precisely what appears in Josephus's account: gold, white, linen, silk, violet, scarlet, and "true purple."

By this divinatory method, Mary is assigned the spinning of two threads, the true purple and the scarlet, and we are told that she goes home to begin her task. Whether in fact she leaves for Joseph's house or, as the original manuscript suggests, she and, by extension, the other seven virgins remain in the temple, I propose that what is being described in this sequence are the basics of a group divine-conception ritual. This is one of the most remarkable aspects of this gospel.

First of all, that the elder Elizabeth is part of this cohort—and the possibility that she also divinely conceives her son, John, as part of this weaving ritual—suggests that this conception rite requires the participation of a group of virgins. Here let's recall the earlier Greek tradition, in which the Gerarai formed an intimate circle that supported the Basilinna in her sacred marriage rite with Dionysus. Let's also remember that the Roman Vestal Virgins comprised a cohort of six, and they too may have engaged in a very secretive practice involving divine birth.

---

*"The War of the Jews, or, The History of the Destruction of Jerusalem" (5.5.4), by Flavius Josephus, found online at Project Gutenberg.
†Casting lots was a common divinatory method that used stones, sticks, or sheep knuckles to determine the will of the Divine.

The idea that a divine-conception ritual is being described is further emphasized by the gospel's passing mention that these events are happening "at the time that Zechariah became mute." This refers to the story in Luke 1:5–24, in which Zechariah and Elizabeth are an older couple who, like Sarah and Abraham, and Anna and Joachim before them, have not had a child. We learn that while praying at the altar, the priest Zechariah is told by the divine messenger Gabriel that his wife has conceived a holy child who will inspire many people to turn to God. When Zechariah questions Gabriel about this because both of them are old, the angel tells him that because of his doubts he will be unable to speak until Elizabeth gives birth—and this does come to pass. The Birth of Mary gives the additional detail that after Zechariah is afflicted in this way he is temporarily replaced in his role as high priest by a man named Samuel until he can speak again.

In Mary's gospel, the virgins' "weaving" of the veil is a symbol clearly associated with divine birth, as we found in chapter 2. In the ancient world, weaving was connected with both the virgin mother goddess Neith as well as Persephone, whose process of self-conception was interrupted while she was at the loom. Weaving was also a sacred activity of the Greek virgin priestesses who prepared garments for the statues of Athena and Hera, both aspects of the Virgin Mother Goddess.[1]

Josephus's description of the images that were woven into the temple veil is also very telling: he writes that the temple veil of Jerusalem essentially depicted the manifold universe, from earthly creatures to the starry heavens. I contend that this is because it was announcing that behind it, in the Holy of Holies, dwelled the Creator of that universe. Therefore, I believe that in the Birth of Mary the so-called weaving of the veil actually represents the virgins' mystical inner tantric (i.e., "weaving") process to bring divine beings from the star realms into their wombs and onto the earth plane. As mentioned in chapter 2, the word *tantra* can be taken to mean "to weave together." I am convinced that the deep meaning of the Holy of Holies is that it is the womb of the Great Goddess, which has its earthly manifestation in the wombs of Mary and all the women who participate in the divine-conception ritual.

It seems that each woman is responsible for a different facet or aspect of the rite, symbolized by the "thread" to which she is divinely assigned. I suggest that the colors that Mary picks, scarlet and true purple, are especially significant because they represent the colors of the root and crown chakras, or energy centers, of the body as understood in Eastern traditions.* They are a further sign that she is involved in weaving into being the divinely born child from head to toe. That Mary is given *two* threads also speaks to the weaving of the two strands of DNA that must be taking place at the quantum level in this profound holy ritual of sacred women.

In meditation I additionally received that the scarlet thread also represents the heart chakra, which is sometimes seen as rosy red in color. This tells us that this spinning, this ritual, is being accomplished through the most profound love; and we will recall from chapter 5 that Mary's name essentially means "Divine Love."

The color true purple† is no doubt another reference to the quality of the child she will conceive. As Josephus mentions in the passage above, purple at that time was a color created by the sea—that is, it came from a dye extracted from a mollusk. In classical antiquity this color was expensive to produce and could only be afforded by the very wealthy. It therefore became a symbol of royalty and political authority. The "true" or "royal" purple color is thus a sign that Mary's son Jesus will be a divinely born spiritual king who follows in the royal lineage of David.

As already mentioned, Mary came to be associated with the sea in her title Stella Maris, "Star of the Sea." The ancient Greek tradition equated the sea with the universe through the concept of Okeanos (or Oceanos), the great river or sea that surrounds the Earth, which is in fact the entire cosmos. Therefore the connection of Mary to the sea is really a reference to her association with the universe itself. As noted in chapter 2, this title may indicate an occult understanding that she was working with the star realms or star beings in her conception of Jesus.

---

*I thank Elizabeth Barton for this insight.
†In the Greek this is rendered as *alethinèn porphúran*.

The color purple in this gospel thus foretells her own ascension to full divinity, which will take place as a result of her divine conception and her good works while on the earth plane.

THE SACRED WATERS OF THE WELL

We see other pieces of the divine-birth ritual woven into the text here. At the point where Mary is spinning the scarlet thread, she takes her water jar and goes out to the well to fill it. There she hears a voice that greets her, tells her that the Lord is with her, and informs her that she is blessed among women. She looks around to see where the voice is coming from, becomes frightened, and goes home. Back in her room, she puts the water jar down, takes up the purple thread, sits down, and begins to weave with it. At this point a heavenly messenger stands in front of her, reassuring her not to be afraid. He tells her that she has found special favor with the Lord of all, the universal creator, and informs her that she will conceive by means of the divine Word, the Logos.

There is a great deal to unpack here, so let's go step by step.

Let's first look at Mary's action of spinning the scarlet thread. The Greek verb used for what she is doing, *klotho,* meaning "to spin by twisting fibers," tells us that Mary is engaged in a spinning-inward process, which means she's going into a trance or an open state of consciousness necessary for her to orchestrate divine conception. Her filling a vessel with water at the well alludes to something she drinks to assist her with that process, perhaps a sacred medicine to open her consciousness for this ritual. I would even go so far as to suggest that it is only because she has taken in such special waters that she is able to hear a divine voice pierce the veil of the dimensions.

Taking an intoxicating drink is something we have a precedence for with the Oracle of Delphi. In the writings about that ancient place we find evidence that the prophetesses, who were also divine-birth priestesses, opened their consciousness by drinking the water of the Cassotis spring, which most likely contained a hallucinogenic substance.[2] In my previous work I have shown that the legendary Ariadne and other divine-birth priestesses most likely drank some kind of substance to induce a trance state for their work.[3] Earlier we saw that Anne may have been chewing laurel to induce the open state necessary for her divine-birth ritual to conceive Mary.

We hear that Mary is afraid, which some interpret to be a sign that she has no idea what's happening. But I propose that her fear is a natural part of the profound and intense process into which she willingly enters. Fear is a typical response when people open their consciousness through the use of sacred substances. During the first twelve years of her life Mary was trained in opening her awareness, so I believe that her apprehension instead indicates that she is going into a deeper state than she has ever gone before, as now, at last, it is "showtime" for her and her virgin consorts.

I consider Mary's water jar to be a double reference: it signals that she has drunk a sacred substance, and that the vessel in this case is a symbol of her womb, which she is indeed in the process of filling. Equating people with vessels of the Divine was a religious concept of the time, as can be seen in a number of other biblical references; the concept of sexual chastity was also closely associated with this.* The water vessel is consistently a symbol of the womb throughout the ancient world, going back to Paleolithic times.†

In addition, in Exodus 37:16 we learn that the table in the Holy of Holies contained pitchers for the pouring of sacred offerings such as oil or wine. These vessels were made of pure gold and were dedicated to God, only to be seen by the high priest and used for holy purposes. I propose that the juxtaposition of references to a vessel, to weaving, and to the Holy of Holies in this sequence tells the astute reader that Mary's own "pure golden womb"—which is nothing less than the Holy of Holies itself—is filling with (or "weaving") what will be an offering of monumental proportions that will be poured out to future generations.

The symbolism of the well at which Mary fills her vessel is also

---

*See, for example, 1 Thessalonians 4:4 and 1 Samuel 21:5.
†See Marija Gimbutas's *Language of the Goddess* for various examples of this in the early European archaeological record.

significant, as the presence of women at wells is consistently connected with divine birth, supernatural events, and prophecy across the ancient world. In the Greek tradition, for example, it is at a well that the four daughters of Metanaera encountered the goddess Demeter grieving for her abducted daughter, Persephone. The virgin-birth theme there is associated with these women and the well in three ways: (1) all of these daughters were divine-birth priestesses; (2) Persephone was abducted at the moment she was attempting virginal conception; and (3) the well at which these divine-birth priestesses find Demeter is called Parthenion, or "well of the parthenos"; i.e., the virgin's well. As we saw in chapter 2, *parthenos* is a word often used to denote a divine-birth priestess. The name of the well thus emphasizes the daughters' ability to become virgin mothers.

There are two significant well encounters in the Hebrew Bible and the New Testament that involve divine-birth themes, as well. In Genesis 24:14, Isaac goes to a well where maidens come to draw water and asks God to show him which one will be his wife by this sign: She will offer water not only to him, but to his camels, as well. Rebecca fulfills that sign, and the two become betrothed. Recall that Isaac himself was the divinely born son of Sarah. As I discussed in chapter 4, the Hellenistic Jewish philosopher Philo states that Rebecca was one of four founding Jewish matriarchs who engaged in a kind of virgin-birth practice.

In the New Testament, Jesus encounters a woman from Samaria at a well. He breaks custom not only by speaking openly with a female in public, but also by taking a drink from her despite the fact that she's from a culture not favored by the Jews. He raises eyebrows because he chooses to speak with a "fallen woman," as well. It is here that he reveals his special holy status as a divinely born son, in part by demonstrating his prophetic skills. Without knowing this woman he stuns her by telling her that he is aware that she has had five husbands and that she is currently with a man with whom she is not betrothed (John 4).

Mary's encounter with the messenger at the well is therefore highly significant. It tells us that she is connected with the lineage of divine-birth priestesses going back to Sarah. It also tells us she will be linked forward in time to a divinely born prophet, Jesus, who will prove to be an evolutionary presence on the planet. It is noteworthy that this particular "well moment" foreshadows one where Jesus demonstrates his visionary powers while attempting to break down restrictive cultural judgments around women's sexuality.

INWARD SPINNING AND WEAVING

That the visit of the divine messenger at the well takes place precisely when Mary has begun to spin the first thread, the scarlet one—that is, the root chakra element—is significant. In women, the root chakra is located in the vagina, so this chakra is connected with the womb. Josephus further tells us that the scarlet thread represents the element of fire, and this corresponds with the kundalini fire that is activated from the root chakra, an energy that is sexual in nature. Recall from chapter 2 the sexual experience of the Muse on the mountain who desired herself to conceive a child parthenogenetically.

I therefore suggest that Mary's spinning refers to a process that not only takes her into a trance state, but that also helps her generate the inner erotic fire energy necessary for the ritual of divine conception. This is another key moment in the gospel where we can understand Mary in a new way. She is not a bloodless maiden; she must rouse raw sexual power within herself for what she is doing.

What I have additionally received is that her spinning refers to the process of going into the void; that is, the quantum sphere of creativity where all manifestation is possible. To create in this space requires erotic energy. I intuit that this erotic fire energy is also related to the light that Claire Heartsong says was part of these divine conceptions. The generation of fire/heat results in the emitting of photons of light on the most profound quantum level in and around Mary's womb and the subsequent special ovum that will pull in the divine child. Photonic light is the equivalent of consciousness itself. So the process she is engaged in is one that involves the human body, the elements, the phenomenon of light, and the phenomenon of consciousness, both hers and its interface with cosmic consciousness.

After Mary enters the spinning/trance/erotic fire process, fills her "vessel," meets the messenger, and goes back home, she next sits down and begins to work with the other thread, the royal purple. The item she is said to sit down on is described as a *thrónos* in ancient Greek, which has been innocuously translated in most editions as a "chair" or "seat." However, the very clear and unequivocal translation of that word in most dictionaries is "throne." In the New Testament the throne is assigned to kings, to Jesus, and to the Divine, hence it is a signifier of royal and divine power. I believe the reference to a throne is both further proof of Mary as a high-level priestess who commands divine power and a description of her womb. The terms *lap, throne,* and *womb* often appear interchangeably in the ancient world. Therefore with this symbol I believe the author of the gospel is saying that Mary's royal womb is the precise location of her activity at this stage of her ritual.

The throne reference may also be pointing to the actual location of these events. In exploring the oldest existing version of the Birth of Mary, religion scholar George Zervos has determined that the throne on which Mary sits must have been the throne of God in the Holy of Holies in the temple. This telltale detail apparently escaped the notice of the zealous editor of this gospel, who was determined to relocate the announcement of Mary's pregnancy outside of the temple.

Zervos and another religion scholar, Michael Peppard, have concluded that the well that is referenced in this sequence in the Birth of Mary may have represented the spring or laver in the temple courtyard, a location commonly associated with supernatural events.[4] So again it may very well be that these events are taking place not in Mary's room in Joseph's house, but in the temple itself.

We now move on to Mary's action with the royal purple thread. The verb used to describe what she's doing with that thread here is *heilko,* "to draw through, with a tugging or stretching motion." That means Mary has now gone from spinning to drawing the thread back and forth. Here is where we understand that she is fully engaged in the metaphorical weaving process. What I understand about this is that Mary's consciousness has moved from the void state of all possibilities, to the stage of pulling through a specific soul imprint into physical incarnation. This is the place in the ritual where she is working with the imprint of her sacred child's DNA to manifest in one of her eggs its blueprint from head to toe. Perhaps, as one of my author colleagues Maura McCarley Torkildson has intuited, at this stage her consciousness is "stepping out of her body" and then back into it, bringing with her the new spirit she is weaving into her womb.

At this point the divine messenger, presumably the same one whose voice Mary heard at the well, appears before her in her chamber. A bit later in the gospel he is identified as Gabriel. That Mary can now see him, in addition to hearing his voice, affirms that she has traveled even more deeply into the inner dimensions in her open state of consciousness in order to accomplish the intricate and profound work she is undertaking at this stage of the ritual. Gabriel reassures her that she has nothing to fear and tells her that she has found favor with the Supreme Creator. He then informs her she will conceive through the Logos, the Word of God.

UNION WITH THE SOUL OF THE UNIVERSE

What does it mean to conceive through the Logos? The Logos is a complex concept in the ancient world, one with multiple meanings. We can start with the more Christianized view, because there's already something there for us. In several passages in the writings of John, the term *Logos* denotes the Word of God in the sense of God's power as Creator of the universe—a power that can also be united with personally.* Here we are talking about *word* not in the grammatical sense of embodying an idea, an object, or a statement. Rather, the Logos is language, or going further, *vox;* that is, sound itself in the form of the wisdom of the Divine transformed into speech or vibration. This is why Mary is sometimes depicted in paintings as conceiving through her ear, as we see, for example, in Fra Angelico's *Annunciation.*

But there is something even more to the Logos beyond mere sound and beyond any notion of a single (male) God. According to the Greek

---

*See John 1 and 1 John 1.

philosophical folks known as the Stoics, the Logos was nothing less than "the soul of the universe." The Merriam-Webster dictionary draws on a similar ancient understanding to define it as "the divine wisdom manifest in the creation . . . of the world." So the Logos signifies a huge universal power.

What is suggested here is that Divine Wisdom is in fact a feminine divine essence known in the ancient world as the Hebrew *Hochmah* (or *Chokhmah*), or the Greek Sophia. Sophia appears in various biblical and extracanonical texts as both an archetypal energy (in the sense of an ultrasmart intelligence and knowing) and a personified goddess who is the embodiment of that knowing. In the Hebrew Bible she holds a high status as the feminine counterpart of God, or Yahweh.* And as feminist scholar Angeleen Campra shows, Sophia is understood to be a Virgin Mother Goddess.[5]

Song comes back into this feminine mix in a telling way with Rudolf Steiner, who equates the Logos with what he calls the "harmony of the spheres," an essence that "permeates space and pours into beings." Even more fascinating: Steiner asserted that it was this very Logos, or cosmic sound, that initiates of Isis experienced when they advanced to the point that they were able to comprehend the goddess Isis in all of her depth. Steiner says this moment was experienced as an inner birth.[6] So essentially Steiner affirms that one's soul rings with the overtones of the feminine universe when one merges with the Sophia/Isis, and this is a profound moment of self-birth/self-conception. In such a process, uniting with the erotic creative force of the cosmos means coming into full marriage; i.e. merging, with the Goddess—the Goddess of which one is already an emanation.

Putting it all together, we can interpret the Logos as the feminine soul song of the universe, which is in everything.

As we saw in chapter 5, Mary herself was already considered an embodiment of Sophia/Isis. So when Gabriel tells her that she will conceive through the Logos, the subtext is that she will be drawing on her very own power as an incarnation of the Divine. This is a

---

*See book of Proverbs 3:13–26 and 8, Wisdom of Solomon 7, and Ecclesiasticus 24.

power that contains the all—both the masculine and the feminine—within her. This recalls the Muse on the mountain, who must generate sufficient desire within herself to become both male and female to conceive.

We can therefore interpret this one word, Logos, as a sign that Mary's conception will be parthenogenetic, one that will be achieved through some kind of unification with the divine creative sound, the divine order, the wisdom essence of the universe. She is literally going to become one with the soul of the universe and, through that erotic encounter, become pregnant.

I believe this passage from the Birth of Mary is also showing us a further technology involved in the divine-conception ritual, in addition to the use of fire/erotic heat and light: the use of sacred sounding or toning on the part of the priestess, a toning that unites her with the soul of creation. This sound of creation has been rendered in Eastern traditions as the great OM, and to this I would add the great MA, the Great Mother. In fact, both of these seed syllables are found in Mary's original name, Mariám, which can be broken down into Ma-Ri-Am = OM. We will see later how she used this sound technology when the high priest states that part of her sacred work involves her hearing the hymns of the heavenly messengers and dancing for them.

MARY DOUBLE-CHECKS

The Greek word to describe Mary's response upon hearing Gabriel's words is *diekréthe,* which some scholars have translated as "she was doubtful." This has been taken to mean that Mary doesn't understand what's going on, and that she is a passive vehicle to this conception process. Given all of what we've explored thus far suggesting the contrary, I believe this is another one of those places where the gospel is concealing what it just dramatically revealed, by offering something that could be seen to slightly downplay her agency. This could also be a place where a later editor may have inserted his hand.

We are required to look deeper, however, because "she was doubtful" is only a superficial translation. The infinitive of the verb, *diakrino,* means "to discriminate, distinguish, decide, judge thoroughly." I propose that Mary is not doubting the message that she will conceive in an unusual way, but rather she is simply double-checking to make sure all is going according to plan. Her specific question in this regard is: "If I conceive by the Lord, the living God, will I also beget a child as every woman begets a child?"*

It's important to note that Mary's question is significantly different from the one attributed to her in Luke 1:34. There, in response to Gabriel's announcement of her pregnancy, she asks, "How will this be, since I am a virgin?" This is a deliberate attempt to obscure her agency in the process, making it appear as though she is essentially a victim to what is taking place. In the Birth of Mary, her question is far more ambiguous. I contend that her gospel is telling us that she is not confused about getting pregnant because she is a virgin. Her question, rather, is a means of seeking confirmation that the conception will not take place as it does for ordinary women; that is, by means of sexual intercourse. In short, she's making sure that she'll retain her sacred virginity in the conception process, confirming that she'll fulfill her role as a holy parthenos, a divine-birth virgin, and that she's not being called on to give birth to an ordinary human child through the ordinary process.

Gabriel reassures her, confirming that the conception is happening through the power of God "overshadowing" her.† By putting the idea of overshadowing together with the fact that she will conceive by means of the Logos, we can read that what has taken place has been an infusion of divine creative universal intelligence into Mary's womb. The messenger is clear that as a result of this divine conception, "the child to be born will be called holy, son of the Most High"—that is, this child will be an avatar, a walking representation of the Divine on Earth, as is the case for all children born this way.

---

*The Greek for "will I also beget a child as every woman begets a child" is *kai gennéso hos pasa gunè genna*.
†The Greek word for "overshadowing" is *episkiazó*.

THE SACRED NAME OF JESUS

Gabriel then instructs Mary to name her child Jesus (in Greek, Iesous; in Hebrew, Yeshua), stating that the name means "he will save people from their hamartia." As already noted, in ancient Greek, *hamartia* means "missing the mark," and although this is often translated as "sin," it really means something more forgiving in the sense of "loss because of not hitting the target." Along these lines, the Hebrew version of this name, Yeshua, is based on a Semitic root meaning "to deliver; to rescue."

What does "missing the mark" mean in this context? I believe it refers to more than mere personal mistakes or character deficiencies; it refers to something much deeper—what the Eastern traditions refer to as *karma*. Karma is another complex (and much-debated) concept, but essentially it's the principle of cause and effect, the idea that the intent and actions of a person influence his or her future in both the present life and future incarnations—in other words, the idea that what goes around comes around. Gabriel is revealing that Jesus's works will involve helping people release lifetimes of "missing the mark." He will help them be absolved of their bad choices and negative actions that have created karmic consequences, perhaps without their even being aware of the concept of karma. In his ministry he will energetically take on the consequences of others' deeds so they may be freed of the endless wheel of rebirth and lifetimes of ever-deepening suffering.

But this will be no mere "forgive and forget" wiping clean of people's slates without their involvement. Jesus and his holy retinue will bring forth tools to help many human beings awaken their consciousness and embrace a higher level of love-based ethics so that their souls will earn and maintain this gift of transformation.

MARY AS TANTRIC PRIESTESS

Mary responds to Gabriel's revelation by saying that she prays that it will all go as it is being presented to her, declaring that she is the "*doule* of God." *Doule* has been translated as "servant," "handmaiden," or even "slave." Thus Mary is affirming what we have known all along, even from before her birth: she is in holy service.

But there is more. The choice of the term *doule* is extremely important because it is part of another ancient Greek word with a religious connection to sexuality: *hierodoule*. This is commonly translated as "holy servant" or "temple servant/slave," and in ancient Greek writings it is used in a few instances to refer to temple priestesses who engaged in sex with men who solicited their services as a dedication to the goddess Aphrodite.*

I interpret from these writings that by the time of the Greco-Roman period this type of sacred sexual service had become a form of temple prostitution in which the monies earned were given to support the temple. Based on my research, however, I believe the original practice was based on sacred marriage—and by extension it involved divine birth.

Bear with me as we tease through my argument here, because it's a bit detailed but will yield something very fruitful and fascinating for us in this discussion. This will be a deeper dive into the world of the temple virgins than we have explored thus far, one that will further illuminate the role of the "virgin daughters of Israel" and Mary's relationship to them.

In Hebrew, the word that conveys the same concept as the Greek *hierodoule* is *qedesha,* which is the term for a female temple sex servant. Like hierodoule, the Hebrew qedesha also contains the linguistic root that means "to be holy," the Semitic stem *qdsh*.† Yes, as we will soon see, the Bible tells us that there were indeed sacred sex servants in Hebrew temples.

Going further with this, we see that this root, qdsh, can also be found in the Akkadian word *qadishtu,* which translates as "hierodoule consecrated to the goddess Ishtar." This means that in ancient Mesopotamia a qadishtu was a sacred sex priestess in service to this

---

*See the description by Greek geographer and historian Strabo (8.6.20) of such hierodoules at the Temple of Aphrodite at Corinth.
†For references to the discussion in this and subsequent paragraphs, see Lapinkivi, "Sumerian Sacred Marriage," 19 and n6; and Nyberg, "Sacred Prostitution," 305–20.

goddess. I propose the Hebrew qedesha was originally a sacred sex servant, perhaps in service to Asherah or Ashtoreth, goddesses whom biblical writings say were still being venerated by the early Hebrews. Let me emphasize that we are talking about holy personnel throughout the ancient Middle and Near East who engaged in sex as part of their sacred role.

In the Sumerian culture, an overlapping neighbor of the Akkadian culture, the term for this type of sexual priestess was *n u-gig,* and this is where we start to see the original exalted nature of all of these terms. N u-gig was one of the titles of the goddess Inanna, who was the Sumerian form of Ishtar. This word also appears around 2700 BCE as the title of a very high female priestess: the queen of the First Dynasty in the Sumerian city of Ur. Such a title as applied to a woman of this high royal status no doubt carried with it the same complex meaning it held when it was applied to Inanna.

Here is where it gets particularly interesting. On the one hand, *n u-gig* means "mistress over heaven," one of Inanna's major roles. On the other, it contains a linguistic inflection that refers to something quite different: "a taboo woman/prostitute." Thus, Inanna as n u-gig combined opposites in the domain of sexuality, much like the later gnostic Sophia, who was simultaneously considered to be "the whore and the holy [virgin.]"[7]

As an n u-gig, this first queen of Ur was regarded as the living representative of Inanna. This means that her role mimicked Inanna's. She was no mere temple sex slave. Rather, she held a high-level sexual function. At the same time, her power was a kind of taboo mystery that also embraced the rawness of sexuality, even its depravity.

We'll get back to Mary shortly, but bear with me as we carry this exploration further. We saw in chapter 4 that priestesses of Inanna likely embodied their goddess for sacred marriage rites. As I put forth when we looked at Sarah, this rite was originally meant to produce divine offspring. Such a ritual that resulted in the birth of pharaohs has been recorded in Egypt. Therefore, I propose that this n u-gig queen was a specialized priestess who engaged in the sacred marriage ritual. I also believe that the Akkadian qadishtu, the Semitic qedesha, and the Greek hierodoule originally referred to a priestess who held a corresponding role in later cultures. And even if the practices changed or degenerated, at the very least these titles carry the memory of this holy role.

So let's look at what the Hebrew Bible says about the qedesha. The big book acknowledges her role in the temple but looks on her with utter disdain.* It consistently and disparagingly equates such a woman with the *zonah,* the common prostitute. Deuteronomy 23:17 gives the following warning: "None of the daughters of Israel shall be a qedesha." Immediately afterward, the verse equates the qedesha with a zonah: "You shall not bring the hire of a prostitute [*zonah*] or the wages of a dog [*keleb*] into the house of the Lord your God to pay a vow, for both of these are an abomination to the Lord your God." This is telling us that no man should engage the services of a temple sex slave as a means of making a religious offering (fulfilling a vow). The problem being lamented here is not prostitution per se, but rather the temple sex practices. The priestesses who continued to engage in it are now characterized essentially as low-level streetwalkers. Obviously, such practices must have been going on in Hebrew temples; otherwise the injunction wouldn't have been issued.

What's particularly striking is the phrase "daughters of Israel" used in the context of the "house of the Lord"; that is, the Hebrew temple. We heard this same phrase earlier in Mary's infancy gospel to describe the virgin priestesses whom Anne calls on to purify and train her daughter. I have already discussed the debate over whether such virgin priestesses could have existed in Hebrew temple complexes, and I offered evidence supporting the possibility that they did. Now, in Deuteronomy, we find the juxtaposition of "daughters of Israel" with the role of the qedesha, the sexual priestess. Again, the linguistics of the term *qedesha* imply a holy function.

I suggest that this biblical passage is one more piece of evidence to indicate that "virgin/undefiled daughters of Israel" were indeed operat-

---

*From the inclusion of the male term *qedesh* in Hebrew biblical references, it is clear that at some point men were also installed as temple sex servants.

ing in the Hebrew temples. It may be that these daughters of Israel were in some cases virgins and in some cases sex workers, depending on their role; that is, depending on whether they were meant to bring forth avatars in celibate divine-conception rites or through sacred marriage rites.

Clearly, the Hebrews did not always follow the command in Deuteronomy to stop their temple sex practices. We hear in Hosea 4:14, for example: "I will not punish your daughters when they act like a zonah [prostitute] or your brides when they commit adultery, for the men themselves go with zonot [prostitutes] and offer sacrifices with qedeshot." We can discern from this statement that that some Hebrew women were indeed still serving as sacred temple *qedeshot,* and that Hebrew men were continuing to use the money payment for their services as an offering (or sacrifice) to the temple. That such women are linked in the same breath with prostitutes once again demonstrates the efforts by early Hebrew patriarchs to eradicate an ancient matriarchal practice that continued in their holy spaces.*

To what extent had the activities of the Hebrew qedesha and Greek hierodoule priestesses come off their mooring of divine birth and truly degenerated into a kind of temple prostitution? The answer is unclear. We can assume that the role of divine-birth priestesses engaging in sacred marriage rites would have been threatening to the encroaching patriarchy. Were the biblical accounts an exaggerated indictment designed to dismiss priestesses who once practiced (or still were practicing) divine birth?

The ancient world was clearly ambivalent about divine-conception practices. On the one hand, its religious institutions needed these practices in order to bring through high-level spiritual and political leaders. On the other, these religions had an uneasy relationship with such practices because they represented women's supreme power, a power that ultimately did not require men. It's because of this threat to the patriarchy that these practices were misrepresented, veiled, hidden, and nearly erased from the ancient texts.

Here is something even more relevant to our discussion about Mary

---

*See also Genesis 38:21–22.

as a doule. I bring in the passage in 2 Kings 23:1–4, which details Josiah's virulent attempt to cleanse the Jewish cult of foreign influences. This account tells us that among the many things the king destroyed were the "quarters of the qedeshim," which were the quarters of the female weavers who lived in the temples. Although the term *qedeshim* is the male plural, I agree with scholar Kristel Nyberg, who argues that the female weavers should be counted as part of this group.[8] As we have seen, these weavers were always virgins.

What all this suggests is that the sacred virgin temple weavers were one and the same with the qedeshot, the priestesses who practiced ritual sex. Again, the qedesha's sexuality originally would have been in service only to "weave in" a divine child through the sacred sex rite.

And in this we have the perfect description of Mary: a virgin weaver dedicated to divine conception.

Thus it is significant that in response to Gabriel's announcement of her pregnancy, Mary calls herself the "doule of God." Some have interpreted the reference to mean "slave of God." Even though it's only half of the term *hierodoule,* "the word *doule* itself carries sexual connotations because slaves were considered to be sexually available to their owners," as Nyberg notes.[9] I argue that Mary is not a slave to the Divine in the sense of a passive or powerless beast of burden, but rather a sacred sexual priestess in passionate dedication to the Logos, the Sophia.

Therefore, with this one word, doule, the author of the Birth of Mary is emphasizing that Mary is in a long line of priestesses who have been trained to use their erotic energy for sacred purposes. Whether the roles of the hierodoule and qedesha had degenerated by now or not, Mary herself remains true to the lineage of her female forbears Anne and Sarah. She and the seven virgin weavers of the House of David have managed to maintain the (scarlet/red) thread going back to the ancestral divine-birth servants of God.

THE CONCEPTION ACHIEVED

The Birth of Mary then tells us that Mary finishes her work with the purple and scarlet threads. We can read this to mean that her ritual is now complete, and the pregnancy has occurred. At this point she goes to the high priest. The text doesn't say whether this is Zechariah. If it is indeed Zechariah, that he will speak to Mary in this encounter means his muteness has been lifted. Luke states that this doesn't take place until Elizabeth gives birth to John the Baptist. We will soon see, however, that Elizabeth is still pregnant at this time. Therefore, either the Birth of Mary has a different time line for the restoration of Zechariah's speech, or the high priest Mary is talking to here is Zechariah's temporary replacement, Samuel.

Whoever the high priest is, he praises Mary, declaring that the Divine has extolled her name and that she will be blessed by all the generations on Earth. It is unlikely that a priest would praise a virgin weaver in this extraordinary way if she were simply presenting him with her tapestry work, no matter how remarkable or ornate the handiwork. I propose the gospel is saying that the temple-veil weaving is a symbol of the divine-birth ritual, and that the male temple personnel are aware of this. Indeed, it is Zechariah who originally puts out the call for the virgins to assemble to begin with. This is presumably owing to his own role as the holy prophet he has demonstrated himself to be, and his connection with his own divine-birth priestess "wife," Elizabeth. So the high priest's words of praise are in recognition of the fact that Mary's conception has been successful.

What is also noteworthy about the priest's words is that in contrast to Luke 1:46–49, they are being said *to* Mary, not *by* her, and they honor Mary, not God, for having accomplished this miraculous feat.[10] Once again, the Birth of Mary provides us with a far more female-centric interpretation of events, crediting the women involved as active agents to a much greater degree than the canonical gospels. This is no doubt one of many places in this gospel that irritated the patriarchal powers that be and led them to reject it as being illegitimate.

THE SPINNING WHEEL OF PRIESTESSES

We next hear that Mary, rejoicing that her accomplishment has been acknowledged, leaves to visit Zechariah's wife, Elizabeth, who is also

Mary's relative.* When Elizabeth hears Mary knock, she "tosses aside her own scarlet thread" and greets and blesses the virgin, honoring her with the title "Mother of God." Elizabeth tells her that the baby who is inside her own womb has jumped for joy and blesses Mary.

Hmm . . . Elizabeth is working with the scarlet thread too? Translators have had trouble with this seemingly unusual detail, to the point where some have eliminated it from the manuscript altogether. As Hock notes, these words "are problematic, in that they seemingly place Elizabeth, who is married, among the virgins who were given the task of preparing the threads for the temple veil."[11]

Yes, indeed. As you can probably figure out for yourself by now, this problem is resolved if we draw on everything we have explored so far. Interpreted in light of this extended discussion of divine birth, the details of the scarlet thread and Elizabeth's own pregnancy reveal that she, too, has been part of the eight women in the lineage of David who have been called to weave the temple veil; that is, who have participated in a divine-birth ritual. Although Elizabeth's elderhood is not explicitly stated in the Birth of Mary the way it is in Luke 1, it's implied by virtue of her relationship to the presumably older high priest Zechariah. What is also affirmed in Luke is that she is a holy woman; there we hear she is "righteous in the sight of God, observing all the Lord's commands and decrees blamelessly." Elizabeth's age, holy status, and pregnancy thus put her in the camp of older divine-birth mothers such as Sarah and Anne.

What does her elderhood tell us about the virgins involved in the weaving/divine-birth ritual? Quite simply, that they are not all young. This supports the idea we've been exploring thus far, that divine-birth priestesses remained virgins for much, if not all, of their lives—or at least until they divinely conceived. Given what we've seen with Sarah and Abraham, and Anne and Joachim, we must assume that Zechariah's role with Elizabeth has been as a celibate guardian over her status as a divine-birth priestess, rather than as a conventional husband.

In Luke 1 we hear that Elizabeth becomes pregnant six months before Mary, but the sequence in the Birth of Mary suggests that the

---

*The Greek word here is *sungenída*.

timing is closer. Elizabeth's baby "leaps" in the womb when she greets Mary, and we know the movement of a child in the womb can be felt as early as three to four months into gestation. So it may indeed be that Elizabeth has become pregnant before Mary has. However, the juxta-position of the detail that Elizabeth is working the scarlet thread when the presumably newly pregnant Mary comes to the door seems to be a clue that their conceptions are very much closer in time. I propose they are both the result of the same rite they have engaged in with the other virgins of the line of David.

Indeed, the gospel implies that the work of the priestesses requires their cooperation and coordination with one another. The number eight is significant, because eight women positioned in a circle formation can be seen to create two crosses that meet at a center point. This point is a place that can be seen as the void, the point of universal creation and divine love.* The importance of this geometry in connection with female parthenogenetic creative power can be seen in a special yantra, or tantric geometrical drawing, known as the Sri Chakra Yantra, which the contemporary Indian master Sri Kaleshwar retrieved from ancient palm-leaf manuscripts of India. The particular yantra that he discov-ered (not to be confused with the more popular Sri Yantra) represents the holy womb chakra of all of creation. This yantra has in its central area what he calls the *nada bindu,* a point surrounded by a circle in which two crosses meet to create the effect of the eight spokes.† The number eight thus signals to us that the women have been working collectively in their "spinning" process; that is, their divine-conception ritual. Perhaps not coincidentally, the spinning wheels that would be created centuries later (to replace or supplement hand spinning utilizing distaffs and spindles) typically had eight spokes.

It is fascinating to ponder the idea that Elizabeth and Mary have been involved in the same ritual together, to "weave" holy avatars into

---

*I wish to thank Karen Holmes for teachings that sparked this insight for me.
†This yantra can be seen on the Sri Chakra page on Sri Kaleshwar's website and the cen-tral point can be best accessed through materials made available with the Holy Womb Chakra Teachings course that I offer at SevenSistersMysterySchool.com.

being. This possibility leads us to many intriguing questions about the divine-birth rite. Does the ritual involve all of the women doing the same conception practice, and at the same time? Or might the detail of the women picking colored threads by lot suggest that some of them are designated to hold different "threads" of the ritual; that is, different roles? Is the picking of the scarlet or purple threads a sign that the priestess is to fulfill the ritual all the way to conception, while the picking of other color threads means one is to be engaged in other activities to support the women chosen to conceive?

Clearly, in honoring Mary with the words she does, Elizabeth is acknowledging Mary's superior status and accomplishment in this ritual. While Elizabeth has conceived an avatar, too, Mary has conceived an even more elevated being. There is a qualitative difference being acknowledged here that I believe recognizes Mary's pedigree—and the abilities that go with it—as a divinely conceived daughter herself. Elizabeth is thus recognizing Mary's mastery as the divine-birth priestess par excellence.

ELIZABETH AND ANNE AS . . . SISTERS?

I will now bring in some other fascinating information about Elizabeth from the Islamic tradition, which supports the idea that she and Mary were indeed part of an intimate group that participated in divine conception. In the Qur'an (19:2–15; 21:89–91), Elizabeth's name, like Anne's, never appears, but she is honored as the wife of Zechariah and (as in Luke) is considered to be holy, wise, and exalted by God to a high degree.

Curiously, in the Islamic tradition Elizabeth is said to have lived in the "house of Imran," a name which, as I have discussed, refers to Anne's "husband" Joachim. Whether this literally means Elizabeth lived with Anne and Joachim or whether this is a reference to her simply being part of the same lineage is unclear. What is particularly noteworthy is that in the sacred texts known as the *hadiths* of the Shia branch of Islam, Elizabeth is named Hananah and is identified as none other than a sister of Anne (Hannah).[12] Stop the presses, because no good Catholic girl ever heard about this! Let us also recall our discussion from chapter 4 about the similarities of these names to Hannahanna. The latter was the name of a mother goddess of the Hurrians of ancient Turkey, who was possibly related to the goddess Inanna, and her name may also have come from the Hittite *Hanna,* meaning "grandmother."

By embracing the Islamic elaboration of the story and putting it together with our exploration so far, what we may well have in Elizabeth and Anne are two holy women and blood sisters with nearly the same divine feminine name, a name that may be related to a goddess of sacred marriage; that is, to divine birth. This name similarity suggests that the name Hannah and its derivatives may also be another priestess title, like the name Mary is. More to the point, I propose that it is a Hebrew honorific title for divine-birth priestesses who are part of a lineage of such women—an idea further supported by the fact that the biblical Hannah, whom we looked at in chapter 4, also had a miraculous conception. Also in line with the divine-birth practices we've been exploring, we see that both Anne/Hannah and Elizabeth/Hananah are supported by men who pose as their husbands, but who are really their sacred guardians.

The Islamic revelation of their sisterhood tells us that their miraculously conceived children—Mary and John the Baptist—are in fact cousins, another family tree detail that's missing in the Christian accounts. And that means that John is Jesus's second cousin. This renders the conceptions of Mary, John, and Jesus a divine family affair indeed!

And then there is this: Could the fact that the Islamic names for Anne and Elizabeth are so similar to the Hittite word for "grandmother" suggest that perhaps these sisters were actually meant to conceive as elders rather than as young maidens? Perhaps the literary spin of supposed lamentation about their being too old to have children is a way of partly obscuring their holy role. This literary choice may be either a distortion on the part of a later scribe to diminish them or, as I discussed when introducing this gospel, a veiling on the part of the original author to conceal the mystery that their pregnancies required knowledge of divine-birth practices.

Given that Anne and Elizabeth's role may have been to conceive avatars only in their elder years, we may also ask whether Elizabeth is the only older woman among the eight virgins who "weave the veil." Perhaps the group requires an equal number of both maidens and crones to provide diversity, balance, and wisdom in order for the ritual to work properly. Mary and Elizabeth's close familial relationship underscores the fact that all of the virgins from the House of David are indeed part of a special female lineage that practices together.

It is also worthwhile to consider that there may be another reason why three of the four women discussed so far as having conceived children divinely—Sarah, Anne, and Elizabeth—are able to fulfill their special conception role only in their elder years. By virtue of the female bodily life cycle, they are technically in their menopausal years, the time in life when the activity of the female hormones has calmed down dramatically of its own accord. I intuit that the reduction of the wild hormones of desire actually enables these elder women to more soberly generate erotic energies without being as susceptible to the presence of marauding and seductive male energies invading their inner planes of reality. As discussed in chapter 2, such male energies were often looking to insert themselves into the priestesses' mental fantasies at the erotic/orgasmic moment of conception so as to interfere with the parthenogenetic process, and therefore to generate their own issue in the women. This was a hazard of the trade for such priestesses, and working with erotic energies was more dangerous and a wild card for the younger ones, whose full-force hormones made them more susceptible to such astral-level seductive thought forms— just as ordinary menstrual women are generally more susceptible to erotic pulls than postmenopausal women in everyday life. That Mary, despite being a young, nubile woman, is able to avoid such a trap and still conceive in a parthenogenetic manner affirms the mastery she has attained over her own body, mind, and spirit.

MARY'S SELF-EFFACEMENT

The Birth of Mary tells us that the young virgin responds to Zechariah and Elizabeth's praise with supreme humility. She momentarily "forgets the mysteries" that Gabriel has spoken of, looks to the sky, and asks, "Who am I, God, that every generation on earth will congratulate me?"

The superficial interpretation of this passage is that Mary is a naive maiden who is unaware of her important role. However, I believe this passage conceals the depth of what is actually being revealed. Read another way, her response indicates that Mary embodies the humble character required to bring forth an exceedingly evolved being, for one of the qualities, even prerequisites, of a divine-birth priestess of the highest order is complete lack of ego. This self-effacement is such that the priestess must hold the majesty and profundity of this greatest of mysteries with the lightest of grasps.

ELIZABETH MENTORS MARY

We next hear that Mary spends three months with Elizabeth, during which time her womb continues to grow. Most of the existing manuscripts tell us that these events are taking place when Mary is sixteen, while some report her age as twelve, fourteen, fifteen, and seventeen.[13] The gospel earlier tells us that Mary is twelve when the priests begin questioning whether she should remain in the temple, and the text seems to imply that the events leading to her going off with Joseph have taken place shortly after that. A several-year absence on the part of Joseph seems unlikely, given that he is serving as her guardian, even if reluctantly. So either Mary is a bit older than the text specifies when she leaves the temple, or the manuscript's statement that she is twelve years old when these events happen is probably closer to the truth.

Whatever the case may be, if we consider the possibility that Elizabeth is not only a co-priestess in the divine-birth ritual but also Mary's aunt—a possibility that I embrace—we can understand why Mary would want to stay with her for an extended visit: She has been involved in a very great mystery practice that she has brought to fruition. Few would be able to understand what she's been going through. We can well imagine that Elizabeth is able to provide needed mentoring, comfort, and safety for a much younger woman who clearly requires this kind of nurturing and support at this point. This would be the case whether Mary is still living in the temple, as the older manuscript versions suggest, or living in Joseph's empty house while he is away. Wherever she is, Mary is "alone of all her sex," a unique woman who has accomplished a rare feat. And despite her tremendous maturity and mastery, she is still young. And human. She needs her elders. I imagine her and her aunt integrating all that has happened together, having many conversations, and entering into deep prayer states to provide blessings and anchoring for the gestating divine children in their wombs. I also imagine them engaging in rituals and prayers to help their babies Jesus and John connect with each other energetically even before they are born.

The question arises: Where is Anne in all of this? Things become very interesting if we recall that in the Islamic tradition Elizabeth is said to have "lived in the house of Imran." If we take that at face value, meaning she literally lived in the house of Joachim (and Anne), then we can read that in going to Elizabeth's house, Mary is actually going to the house of her parents. Has this young, holy parthenos been able to find temporary refuge in the home of both divine birth elders in her lineage? This possibility fills the gap as regards Anne's sudden departure from the text* and suggests much about how Mary spent the first three months of her pregnancy and what kind of support she may have received.

THE VULNERABILITY OF MARY

The gospel tells us that as Mary watches her womb growing larger every day, she becomes frightened. At this point she chooses to return home to "hide from the people of Israel."

The mention of fear is generally interpreted as another sign of Mary's lack of agency and awareness in the conception process. However, as we know, the text can be read another way: Rather than being an indication of her passivity and being overwhelmed, we can understand Mary's fear as a natural response that a conscious divine birth-priestess would have in such a situation. Mary is a young woman operating in a world

---

*It is otherwise possible that Anne has died by this time.

in which divine birth is increasingly repressed. In some cases, as seen in the legendary stories of ancient Greece and the historical accounts of Egypt, it has been co-opted by hierarchical, patriarchal, religious, and political institutions. In other cases, it has become a much-diminished practice that's been harnessed for magical purposes, without resulting in a divine conception. In still other cases it has possibly degenerated into a form of temple prostitution.

We can see that for priestesses such as Sarah, Anne, and Mary, who are still attempting divine birth the old way, the authentic practice has had to go underground as a mystery that fewer and fewer people can understand or support. It is veiled even in the texts that talk about miraculous pregnancies, such that today it requires the kind of keen sleuthing we've been doing in this book to even recognize it. At the time when Mary lives, divine conception is extremely threatening to the patriarchy, a manifestation of women's spiritual power that has become increasingly attacked through skepticism, erasure, harassment, and violence.

Mary will encounter all of these responses, as we shall see. Therefore I contend that she needs to hide her situation not only from nosy neighbors who might question the pregnancy of a girl who, as this gospel makes clear, is unmarried and is supposed to remain a virgin. Even more important, she needs to conceal her condition from "the entire nation of Israel" because of the kind of child she carries. Presumably she recognizes she will be too visible in Elizabeth's (and possibly Anne's) household or neighborhood, and her need for hiding overtakes her need for sisterhood and familial nurturing. She decides, perhaps after consulting with her female elders, that it's time for her to leave and move into the next phase of her experience with faith and courage.

IN SUMMARY: WHAT ARE MARY'S METHODS OF DIVINE CONCEPTION?

We've covered a lot of detail in this chapter, so let's take a moment here. What are the main things Mary has done, exactly, to conceive Jesus? The gospel has given us the following clues:

First, she is part of group of eight women who all hail from the same exalted lineage, a cohort that includes her aunt Elizabeth, who is also able to conceive divinely. This suggests that Mary must of necessity be part of a specific bloodline of trained women in order to even begin the process, and that these women somehow all work together.

Second, she is assisted in opening her awareness by drinking some kind of mind-expanding substance, and this allows her to access the inner domains of consciousness needed for her work. This in turn enables her to speak directly with a divine messenger, who is also critically important in guiding the process.

Third, Mary engages in what is metaphorically described as spinning and weaving, which is a reference to some kind of energetic techniques she is using. This results in the generation of kundalini heat or fire in her womb, and a corresponding light that is a form of consciousness itself. It also seems that at the same time she is producing or tuning in to some kind of sacred sound, word, or song of the universe—the Logos.

Fourth, Mary's later title, Stella Maris, "Star of the Sea," conveys the mystical understanding that in her conception rite she also is working with the realm of light in the sense that she is connecting with star beings (the reference to a special star associated with the birth of Jesus is discussed in the next chapter). As noted earlier, clairvoyant Claire Heartsong has affirmed that the divine pregnancies among Mary and the women of her lineage were "light" conceptions. All of this suggests that for the divine-conception process to take place, Mary interacts with the interface of light and matter at an exceedingly sophisticated level.

Fifth, Mary's process is governed by a lack of ego and a wealth of love, for it is ultimately the love element that fuels the entire divine-birth process and makes the conception possible. This is why, as we saw in chapter 5, Mary was given a name that means "divine love." Her name thus represents a prophecy fulfilled.

What is noteworthy about Mary's conception of Jesus, in contrast to Anne's conception of Mary and Sarah's conception of Isaac, is the lack of engagement on the part of Joseph. While Anne is energetically supported by Joachim during his vision quest, and while there are strong signs that Sarah may have been involved in sacred marriage rites with male humans or divinities as part of her divine-birth practice, we see no such parallel situation with Mary. The most we get from her gospel is that she is made pregnant by the Logos, or soul of the universe. This represents the fully parthenogenetic engagement that Mary has with her inner powers as an avatar of the Divine Feminine.

I therefore contend that Mary's specific process tells us that she was the most advanced of all the women who conceived miraculously before her. Her conception of Jesus, in my interpretation, is the most sophisticated example of holy parthenogenesis that we have ever seen. Anne's was a kind of female-producing parthenogenesis, but she had the support of Joachim on some level. What's more, her female-female parthenogenesis was assisted by the biological factor of the X chromosome in her eggs, requiring her to induce meiosis, but not otherwise intervene in the process in any way.

Moreover, in Mary's case, not only does she do it all by herself—for Joseph was clearly disengaged from her—she was able to achieve the seemingly counterbiological feat of producing a male child without the benefit of any kind of sacred marriage rite, even a symbolic one, in contrast to Anne and probably also Sarah. This, to my mind, renders Mary the divine-birth priestess par excellence. She has done it all by herself. Her achievement befits her status as a human avatar and speaks to the industriousness she must have applied to her training. It is owing to this combination of factors that she is able to bring to the planet a being of the level of Jesus.

These are but hints as to what Mary is really up to in her ritual. This exploration leaves us with many more questions than answers, but it allows us to look at the conception of Jesus in a way few have been able to consider before. We will next turn our attention to what life is like for Mary as a young woman who has accomplished the greatest shamanic feat possible, a feat that will shake the foundation of the world in which she lives.

And for you living in today's world . . . the veil that has been placed over Mary's divine conception of Jesus is now lifted. How does this affect you? Is it something that resonates as truth? If so, what does that mean for you? What does Mary's special situation suggest about the potential womb power of all women? Do you want to know more? Have you received your own information on this that has come to you in any particular or extraordinary way? Is there anything you'd like to share? Or . . . are you still ruminating? Let us hear from you on the Seven Sisters Mystery School Facebook page.

CHAPTER 7

Mary's Trials and the Birth of Jesus

From here onward, the Birth of Mary tracks our blessed heroine through a series of challenging happenings leading up to the birth of Jesus. We will witness the accusations she endures about her pregnancy, travel with her on the trips she and Joseph must undertake, and come to understand the remarkable prophetic visions the two of them experience just before Mary gives birth to Jesus in a cave.

We will then traverse the dangerous terrain she and the other members of the extended Holy Family must negotiate as they are hunted down by the authorities. This includes Elizabeth, who must flee with her divinely born son, John; and Elizabeth's companion, Zechariah, who meets a gruesome end for having steadfastly refused to reveal John's whereabouts. This will bring us to the end of Mary's gospel and its coda, in which the author reveals how he received the inspiration of the Divine Feminine to write while in exile.

A DOUBTING JOSEPH

Mary's troubles as a virgin-birth priestess who has conceived a child without the help of a man begin in the sixth month of her pregnancy. That's when Joseph finally comes home from his building projects only to find her belly swollen with child. He is beside himself with shock. He strikes himself in the face, throws himself on the ground, and begins to cry, asking, "What prayer can I say on her behalf since

I received her as a virgin from the temple of the Lord and didn't protect her?"

It seems that Joseph is finally taking responsibility for having skipped town and fallen down on his duties as Mary's protector. He continues lamenting, saying that she must have been violated, in the same way Eve was corrupted by the serpent. But he quickly shifts his blame to Mary. He chastises her for bringing shame on herself, declaring that her embarrassment should be all the more extreme given that she was raised in the "Holy of Holies and fed by a divine messenger."

Here, Joseph is revealing to us something that we have not exactly heard before—that during her training Mary had access to the part of the temple usually reserved only for the high priest. This affirms something we've been considering all along: that Mary was recognized as a priestess of the highest order. And what does this mean? I believe that in telling us this, and in reiterating that she received special "food" from the divine messenger that we talked about in chapter 6, Joseph is acknowledging Mary's training as a divine-birth priestess.

Apparently he does not yet consider that her pregnancy could be a miraculous one. This shows us that he has his doubts that such a thing could even be possible, a lack of faith we saw earlier in Zechariah when he was presented with the miraculous nature of Elizabeth's conception. This is why we learn from Luke that when Zechariah questions Gabriel about the pregnancy because he and Elizabeth are old, the angel tells him that he will be stricken with muteness because of his doubt.

Zechariah's doubt and Joseph's outburst tell us that even these men who are supposed to serve as guardians of divine-birth priestesses cannot fully hold to their higher consciousness around what is happening. Their third-dimensional minds are getting in the way of higher-dimensional realities concerning these siddhis, the seemingly biology-defying abilities that are possible when an advanced master fully engages in the realm of Spirit. This doubting is apparently perceived in the divine realm as a failure in their roles as guardian consorts—and certainly in the case of Zechariah that message is clearly delivered by the higher-ups when he loses his ability to communicate for a time.

Even Joachim had his doubts—he had to double-check that Anne's conception was truly divine by asking for a sign in order to believe. By looking into the polished disc of the priest's headgear, he was granted that reassurance: the immediate understanding being that "there was no violation of divine law" in what he and Anne had done. So he was telepathed by divine forces that the conception was indeed a result of their collaboration in the divine-birth rite. He could then rest easily.

At this point in Mary's gospel, Joseph is not quite there yet. He declares in dramatic tones that just as the evil serpent visited Eve while Adam was in prayer, so he himself has had evil afflict his house—and all this despite the fact that he has been a devout man.

In the face of Joseph's carryings-on, Mary cries bitterly, declaring she is *katharå,* a word translated as "innocent," but that actually means several things, among them, "unstained, either literally or ceremonially or spiritually." I believe Mary is not so much defending her honor as a virgin in the conventional sense but rather reassuring Joseph that she has retained her ritual status as a holy virgin. She then blatantly declares that she has not had sexual relations with any man.

Joseph nevertheless continues to interrogate Mary, asking her where, then, has the child come from? In the gospel, Mary responds: "As the Lord my God lives, I do not know where it comes from." I believe this is another case in which the text is revealing and concealing at the same time. Taken at face value, a statement like this might be seen as yet another indication that Mary has not been an active agent in her conception of Jesus. But taken another way, it might simply mean that even a divine-birth priestess cannot determine precisely which domain the soul of her child hails from.

We can imagine Mary's feelings of shock and even betrayal at being treated by Joseph like this. The human Mary is not in Kansas anymore, so to speak—no longer in the protected bedroom of her mother, the cloistered environment of the temple, or the nurturing home of her aunt. She is now a young woman out in the world, seeing how the three-dimensional world is responding to her hard-won accomplishment. Her first welcome to this world is a symbolic slap. It's not going to be an easy road.

After hearing Mary's adamant assurance of her ritual purity, however, Joseph becomes afraid. There is something far more to all this, he realizes. He goes away in silence to ponder what he will do. Out pours from him a soliloquy in which he admits to being uncertain as to whether the child has been conceived through relations with a man, or whether it might indeed be "a divinely sent messenger" (*angelikón*). This deliberation indicates that he is indeed acknowledging Mary's capability to conceive through divine means. I contend, however, that although he recognizes her to be a specialized priestess who has been raised in the Holy of Holies, he doesn't know her well enough to be able to vouch for her integrity. And how could he? He no sooner took her into his home as his charge than he went off on an extended trip.

Joseph is caught in a bind as to whether he should either (1) cover it all up and risk sinning in the eyes of God if indeed Mary has faltered; or (2) expose the situation publicly and leave it up to the community to decide. He fears that if he goes public, he risks her child being killed for what is likely to be seen as Mary's violation of her sacred virgin role. This tells us that he is aware that people could not understand or accept the mystery of divine conception, and that they would assume what most ordinary folks would assume: that her pregnancy was the result of an ordinary sex act.

Joseph comes up with a different solution. The word used here for what he decides to do is *apoluó,* which is sometimes translated as "to divorce," and this is how it has generally been translated by scholars of this gospel. But there has been no marriage. That there was no betrothal emerges later, when Joseph is accused of having had sexual relations with Mary and is publicly punished for it. Therefore, I believe the other translations for *apoluó* are more accurate—namely, that Joseph is going to "dismiss," "discharge," "release from a bond," or "set free" Mary. Without anyone knowing, he is going to quietly disengage himself from his agreement to be her guardian and walk away from the whole thing.

That night, Joseph is stopped dead in his tracks. A divine messenger comes to him in a dream, telling him not to be afraid of Mary because the child in her is indeed from the Holy Spirit. The word the messenger uses to refer to Mary is *paida.* In its simplest translation it means "girl." But it also has another meaning, "servant," with the implication being that she is a servant of the Divine. In its masculine form it is one of the titles of Jesus, signifying "an upright and godly man whose agency God employs in executing his purposes."

Once again the gospel is both revealing and concealing Mary's status here. On the one hand, it presents her as a simple maiden who has no idea why she is pregnant. On the other, it offers a code word that indicates her status as a special divine "servant" whose child will hold a similarly exalted title. I believe that by following the double meaning of the word *paida,* the author of the gospel is suggesting that she is a divine-birth priestess who knows exactly what she is doing.

The divine messenger reiterates to Joseph what he revealed to Mary about the future name of the child. Greatly relieved, Joseph gets up from his sleep and praises God for granting him this grace. It is here that the gospel tells us that Joseph finally accepts his responsibility as a protector of Mary. Until now he has basically been ditching his duties and using work as an excuse. With the proof at hand that Mary has fulfilled her mission as an authentic priestess of the highest level, he is at last stepping up to his preordained role.

WORD OF THE PREGNANCY GETS OUT

Joining forces with Mary soon brings its challenges, however. A meddling scholar named Annas comes to Joseph's home to chide him for not having been present at a public assembly. Joseph explains that he was too exhausted from his trip to attend. During this unexpected visit, Annas encounters Mary and sees that she is pregnant. Horrified, he immediately scurries over to the high priest to accuse Joseph of having "violated the virgin he received from the temple of the Lord." Joseph's worst fear about what could happen to Mary if her pregnancy is exposed is now about to manifest.

Annas's actions and words tell us several things. Mary and Joseph are not married, because otherwise no one would question Joseph's right as a husband to have relations with his wife. They also imply that even though Mary is (according to this version of the gospel) no longer living in the temple and having access to the Holy of Holies, her service as a virgin is expected to be long-standing. This was the case for Sarah and Anne, and now Mary's situation illustrates this more clearly.

Annas's words echo Joseph's earlier fears, that the revelation of a temple virgin's violation of her vow of chastity would incur public wrath and a demand for punishment. This recalls the gruesome reality in Rome around this time, where a Vestal Virgin could be buried alive if found guilty of having violated her vow of chastity. All of this is to suggest that ancient holy virginity requirements were far more than just a means of privately controlling the behavior of women. They seem to have also been a means of harnessing female womb energy and redirecting it to energetically "feed" entire populations. The energy of Mary's untouched womb—along with those of Anne, Elizabeth, Sarah, and her virginal sister priestesses—was considered by the broader world beyond the Hebrew temple as nothing less than a form of energetic sustenance for the people. Any disruption of that container, that holding, and that feeding could provoke a rage among the people akin to that of an infant denied the breast.

MARY UNDER FIRE

The high priest is deeply concerned about Annas's accusations. He sends temple attendants to the home of Joseph and Mary to round them up for questioning in the temple court. Although his identity is not specified, we know the priest must either be Zechariah, if his speech has by now been restored, or Samuel, who is substituting as high priest if Zechariah is still mute.

Whoever the priest is, his actions could be read as implying that he is unaware of Mary's pregnancy. However, we know this is not the case, because earlier he verbally glorified Mary, declaring that she would be honored worldwide for all future generations. Such over-the-top praise could only have been a recognition of her divine pregnancy, not her loom work. I believe that once again the gospel is both exposing and hiding the truth. Part of the priest's problem is that he knows the pregnancy has now been revealed to a public that is not privy to temple mysteries. He also knows that despite public ignorance of secret doings, the community needs to be placated in its desire to know whether a temple virgin violated her vow. And he understands that the people need to be satisfied in their desire for retribution if this is the case.

I believe the priest's concern is not over whether Mary is pregnant but over something more grave: namely, whether Joseph could have interfered with the conception. He wants assurance that this pregnancy was indeed divinely, not carnally, accomplished. This is the real reason he sends out the scouts and subjects Mary and Joseph to the extreme methods that we will hear about shortly. This is all the more the case if the priest is Zechariah, who would have recently housed Mary for three months. Recall that his "wife," Elizabeth, openly recognized Mary's divine pregnancy, so clearly Zechariah would have had that reality in his face for three months as well.

At this point, the scouts round up Mary and Joseph and bring them to the temple court. The high priest begins to harass Mary, essentially accusing her of having had sexual relations with Joseph. He asks her why she has humiliated herself in this way and whether she has forgotten her agreement with God. Clearly he is putting the screws on her to test her level of truth telling. Echoing Joseph, he reminds her that she has been "raised in the Holy of Holies" and has been "fed by heavenly messengers."

This is the second time in Mary's gospel that we hear that she has had access to the Holy of Holies. Again, this is code for her advanced status as a high holy woman and a divine-birth priestess. An interesting detail the high priest adds that we have not heard before emphasizes this: he says that Mary "heard the hymns of these heavenly messengers" and "danced for them."

What could this mean? Well, let's recall earlier that Mary began her tenure at the temple by dancing on the steps when she was three years old. Her ability to do so was owing to the specific training she received from the virgins who had been preparing her for her destiny as a divine-birth priestess from the time she was still in her mother's sanctuary. The priest's statement therefore tells us that Mary has continued this "dancing" practice at the temple—a practice that I believe refers to a special aspect of her training in divine birth connected to her hearing heavenly hymns.

Recall that we said earlier that Mary's pregnancy was the result of her connection with the Logos, the divine word, the sound of the universe, or great OM. This most likely refers to the possibility that Mary was working with sound technologies as part of her divine-birth practices. Now the priest's mention of heavenly hymns does indeed seem to be referring to the special sound frequencies on the inner dimensions in which she engaged. His statement implies that Mary practiced with this technology throughout her entire time at the temple as part of her prep work for divine conception.

The priest's shaming of Mary is quite driving here. I believe his intensity reflects his worry over Annas's accusation that Mary's pregnancy was caused by Joseph. What if she misrepresented herself when she presented her temple veil work, that is, her divine conception, six months earlier? What if she is carrying not a divine child, but a child of a human man? It seems the stakes are high, and I would imagine this is the case because of the extreme care and effort that must have gone into the divine-conception ritual on the part of all the sacred personnel who were involved in it or who supported it.

Stunned by the accusations, Mary weeps bitterly and declares that she has not had sexual relations with any man. We can imagine Mary's trauma at being harangued in such a public way by a high official. The energies are now clearly intensifying, and we can imagine her fear, despite the fact that she is a young master. The priest then presses Joseph, asking why he has violated Mary, and he, too, proclaims his innocence. The priest bears down harder, warning Joseph not to perjure himself and telling him that his violation has been particularly great because he has not confessed what he has done publicly. What's more, he has not humbled himself before God so that he may be forgiven and the child can be embraced by the community.

MARY'S GREAT TEST

The high priest then tells Joseph that as a result of these sorry doings he must turn Mary over to the temple. We can well imagine that placing Mary under custody and at the mercy of a public who will be enraged about an avowed virgin who has become pregnant would put her and her child in grave danger, just as Joseph feared. Upon hearing this judgment, Joseph bursts into tears. We can only imagine what Mary herself must be feeling at this moment.

Joseph's display apparently moves the priest, because the high official does not take Mary back to the temple after all. Instead, he tries another tack to get at the truth. He tells both of them that he is going to subject them to "the water of the rebuking of the Lord,"* which he declares will clearly result in the disclosure of their wrongdoing. This may refer to something like the strange ritual of the "water of bitterness" for unfaithful wives that is described in Numbers 5:11–31. There we hear that if a husband is suspicious that his wife has had sex with another man, he can bring her to the temple priest to wrest the truth out of her. The priest forces the woman to drink a potion of "bitter water." This water contains a heinous curse he has put on it: If she has indeed been unfaithful, her belly will swell and she will abort the child. If nothing happens, she will be cleared of guilt.†

The process is a bit different in the Birth of Mary, however, in that both Joseph and Mary are required to drink this water, the implication being that both will be harmed in some way if they are lying. This is yet another place where the gospel is more feminist in orientation than other texts of its day in that it is not only the woman who is being given the third degree.

Our Hebrew high priest is not alone in facing such a dilemma. Claims of ritual virginity and divine conception often provoked suspicion and the need for proof in the broader ancient world, for how could anyone ever be certain that a priestess had remained celibate, or that her divine conception was authentic?

This is why we see these tests of virginity pop up in the literature associated with divine birth in Greece and Rome. The Roman author Aelian, for example, describes a peculiar tradition carried out

---

*The Greek is *tò húdor tes eléngxeos kuríou.*

†See also the Mishnah Sotah 1 for the use of "bitter waters" in dealing with a woman suspected of adultery.

at Hera's cult site in Rome: The virginity of priestesses was verified only if snakes accepted the young women's food offerings. As the townspeople learned of the outcome of the ritual, they would examine the maidens further. Those girls whose bodies (presumably their hymens) revealed that they had violated their virginity were apparently punished by law.[1]

As I show in *The Cult of Divine Birth in Ancient Greece*, it is likely that Hera's cult at some stage included a divine-birth priestesshood. I have suggested that this snake ritual was the vestige of a divinatory practice originally designed to determine which young women were either (1) suited to be divine-birth priestesses in the first place, or (2) dutifully maintaining their virginity for such a purpose. By the late Roman period, however, as Aelian reports, the snake-offering test had degenerated into a ritual to judge and punish a woman who was no longer considered "morally pure."

The Vestal Virgins also at times had to defend their claims of virginity. We know this because of the mention of a particular test that at least one of them had to undergo to prove her chastity, that of carrying water in a sieve. This meant transporting water in a flat, perforated basket without its leaking. Since this is ordinarily impossible, the successful accomplishment of it was thought to be a sign of divine favor. This nerve-racking test was undertaken by a Vestal Virgin named Tuccia, whose chastity was called into question. The priestess beseeched the goddess Vesta for help, asking that she grant her the ability to draw water from the Tiber and bring it to Vesta's temple. According to ancient sources, Vesta answered Tuccia's plea, the priestess miraculously carried the water in the basket without any of it dripping out, and she was absolved of suspicion.[2]

In her gospel, then, Mary is not the only avowed temple virgin of her time to have drawn suspicion to herself. The particular test she is made to undergo requires first Joseph and then her to go out into the wilderness for a time after drinking the bitter water. How long this ordeal takes, and what they are each experiencing in their hearts as it is taking place, we are not told. We only hear that they each humbly make their way back scot-free and unharmed.

Seeing that this is the outcome of the test, the priest changes his tone. He absolves them of any guilt, and they are free to go. His public exoneration implies this: If Joseph did not impregnate this virgin, then God must have. In other words, he recognizes that Mary's child has indeed been divinely conceived, and he tells the community that this is something they are just going to have to accept. She and Joseph return home in celebration.

MARY'S PROPHECY ABOUT JESUS

The gospel now shifts its narrative, telling us that a decree has been issued from the Roman emperor Augustus ordering everyone in Bethlehem of Judea to enroll in the census. This puts Joseph in a quandary. He thinks to himself that it will be easy for him to enroll his sons (recall that he was a widower with children when attached to Mary), but he wonders how he is to categorize Mary. As his wife? He would be ashamed to do so because of their great age difference. As his daughter? No, the community of Israel is aware that she is not one of his children. He throws up his hands and leaves the decision up to God.

Joseph packs for the trip to Bethlehem, saddling up the donkey and setting Mary on it. The gospel tells us that his son leads the donkey, with another man named Samuel (who may be another son) bringing up the rear. Because the first son's name is not specified, Hock says this may be an indirect reference to the author of the gospel, the self-identified James.[3] This is significant because if so, this James will be an eyewitness to the virgin birth to come.

Three miles into the trip, Joseph turns around while walking to check on Mary and sees that she is gloomy and sullen. He guesses this may be because she is feeling discomfort from the baby she is carrying. Not a moment later, he turns around again only to see her laughing. Struck by the abrupt change in the blink of an eye, he questions her about why she is one way one minute and another way the next. Mary replies with an enigmatic comment: "Joseph, it is because I imagine two peoples in front of me, one weeping and mourning, and the other celebrating and jumping for joy."

Various interpretations of this cryptic statement have been suggested,* but I believe it clearly reveals Mary's prophetic understanding of how her divine child will be received. In her journey while traveling across the vast expanse, she no doubt has had time to reflect on events to come. What is being shown to her is that some will see Jesus's messages and presence as a means of bringing joy and healing to their lives and to the world, while others will see them as a source of sorrow and punishment, for themselves and for others.

This is the first time in this gospel that Mary is revealed as an oracle priestess with visionary abilities. She is prophesying a truth that is echoed in the gnostic Gospel of Philip (29): that Jesus will be seen and received according to a person's own vantage point and level of spiritual growth. And as we know, her vision will play out in the personal and political arenas over the next two thousand years. Some will use Jesus's teachings and ministry for personal, spiritual, and even political liberation, while others will use them to judge, enslave, torture, war on, and otherwise harm themselves and others.

It must be a disturbing reality for this young priestess to know that her child, no matter how holy, will be entering the world of matter and duality, and that all those associated with him will have to come to terms with that. In a sense she is, in this very moment, just before she is about to give birth, also able to foresee the circumstances of her son's death, in which the duality around his teachings will be played out in a deeply painful way. Once again, we can really appreciate Mary as a human woman who will have to grapple with maintaining the high vibration of love amidst agony and fear as the events of her son's life unfold.

JOSEPH'S MIND IS BLOWN

Halfway through the trip, Mary goes into labor. At this point we can figure she must be nine months pregnant, although it is not fully clear from the gospel how long her virginity test took or how long she's been

---

*See, for example, Hock's *Infancy Gospels,* 63 n17:9.

traveling. Given that Joseph returned to her when she was six months pregnant, these two events must have unfolded in three months' time.

Since the little caravan is exposed in the open plain where they travel, Joseph finds a cave on their route and takes Mary inside. This is different from what we find in Luke 2:7, where Jesus is born in the stable of an inn, or Matthew 2:11, where Jesus is born in the house of Joseph and Mary. The setting in the Birth of Mary could not be more appropriate and, I would add, more accurate. Caves are known worldwide, going back to ancient times, as places of birth, death, and initiation. A cave is literally the womb of Mother Earth, in which this priestess, as a manifestation of the Great Mother, will give birth. Once again we find that Mary's gospel seems to be more attuned to female-centered realities than the canonical gospels.

Joseph stations the two young men who have accompanied them nearby to guard Mary and goes searching throughout the countryside around Bethlehem for a midwife to assist her. We do not know how long he is gone, and it may be a considerable period of time, because we are told of an uncanny experience he has while on his quest, something that suggests he has perhaps been influenced by the elements to go into an altered state of consciousness. Here, for whatever reason, the narrative temporarily shifts to first person, so we now hear the story in Joseph's own words.

He tells us that he suddenly finds himself in a strange, dreamlike reality: he is both walking along, yet frozen in place. Just as he finds himself suspended in time, the sky above him stands still, the clouds "paused in terrifying, wondrous amazement," the birds hanging in mid-air. Looking down, he sees a bowl lying on the ground with workers reclining around it. They are in various stages of having their hands in the bowl, picking up something to eat and chewing—yet at the same time they are not doing those things. Instead they are all looking upward. Joseph then sees sheep being driven along yet standing still, a shepherd lifting his hand as if to strike them, yet his hand remaining raised. He observes the current of the river and sees goats with their mouths in the water, yet not drinking. Then, in a flash, everything resumes as normal.

Joseph's vision describes what I believe is an experience in which he has transitioned from third-dimensional consciousness to fourth-dimensional consciousness, a domain where time is the featured element. We are shown the simultaneous nature of time and that time is paradoxical. Joseph is experiencing what many esoteric traditions have shown, an understanding that has been verified by quantum physics in recent decades: that all things take place at the same time, even though in our present dimension things appear to happen in a linear, sequential fashion.*

In his vision Joseph also perceives that motion and stillness are one. He is being shown the realm of nonduality—one is two, and two are one. His experience of unity consciousness is a companion piece to Mary's vision of the realm of duality. Both of their visions demonstrate how Jesus will be affected by understandings of the nature of reality, and how his presence in turn will influence those understandings. I believe that Mary and Joseph are being prepared, as are we readers, for what the coming of Jesus will bring: the grappling with extremes, something that is being increasingly dramatized in our world today. They, and we, are being granted an awareness of the need to refrain from fragmenting into duality by courageously holding opposites, not as things that are separate and unrelated, but as polarity aspects of the whole yin-yang enchilada. This will lead us to an understanding that beyond both the physical plane (third dimension) and linear time (fourth dimension), there is another dimension, the fifth, in which we are able to maintain and resolve the tension of opposites through an awakened consciousness that sees all as one and an awakened heart that can forgive the seeming other, the enemy, through radical forgiveness and infinite trust in things as they truly are.

This fifth-dimensional awareness is the realm of "looking up" that Joseph describes, meaning looking *inward* into ever-greater depths into which the Divine will continue to beckon us. It is the realm in which what we consider to be food and drink will shift. The Birth of Mary is

---

*See, for example, Tom Kenyon and Judy Sion's *The Arcturian Anthology* for revelations on the subject of time.

telling us that with the presence of an avatar such as Jesus on the planet, many more will find they will no longer need to live on bread alone. Like the ascetic Therapeutae, whose real food was spiritual ecstasy, and like Mary, who took in special food from the heavenly messengers, far more people will discover a more nourishing inner manna.

Through these partnered visions, then, we can see that for both Mary and Joseph, the very fabric of reality, the "veil of the temple," is becoming quite thin, and their consciousness is thus able to apprehend more and more. This is what the swiftly approaching birth of Jesus is bringing for them personally, and for humanity collectively.

MARY'S "DUELING" MIDWIVES

As his vision dissolves, Joseph spies a woman coming down from the hill country. Clearly this is another synchronistic moment in which the veils of reality are still thin and Joseph is being divinely guided, because the woman is revealed a bit later to be precisely the person he's been seeking: a midwife. Moreover, she asks who is having a baby in the cave, a situation that has not yet been revealed to her. This suggests she is a seer as well.

When the midwife asks Joseph about his relationship to Mary, he tells her that she was raised in the temple, that he obtained her by law, that she is not really his wife, and that she is pregnant by the Holy Spirit. Now we hear in Joseph's own words that he is her sacred guardian, not her husband.

The woman, whose work is all about birthing babies, is curious about someone who has become pregnant in such an extraordinary way. Joseph invites her to come with him to assist. When they get to the cave, a bright light covers the entrance.* The midwife knows this is a sign that a miracle is taking place within, and she expresses gratitude for being witness to the *soteria* that has come to Israel. This word is generally translated as "salvation," but I prefer the alternative meanings: "welfare," "prosperity," "preservation," and "safety." What is being expressed

---

*Hock, *Infancy Gospels,* 67 n19:13, translates this light as "dark cloud," even though he notes that most versions of the manuscript call it a "bright cloud."

here is the promise of nurturing and well-being that Jesus's ministry will offer. Although the midwife has never encountered anything like this in all of her work tending births, she clearly understands what's going on.

When the light that covers the entrance withdraws, another light appears inside the cave, one so bright that the midwife, Joseph, and presumably his sons who are guarding the cave cannot bear to look. The light eventually recedes until the infant Jesus becomes visible and takes the breast of his mother, Mary. As Hock notes, Mary's not needing to wait for the prescribed purification period to nurse her child (in contrast to her mother, Anne) may be a sign of her great spiritual purity.[4] Indeed, we must keep in mind that she is not only a divine-birth priestess but a divinely born person herself, so she is a doubly elevated human being.

The midwife shouts that it has been an exultant day for her because she has witnessed yet another miracle—implying that she has seen two such events, one being a divinely conceived birth, and the other being a birth that did not require a midwife's hand. On her way home she meets a woman named Salome, to whom she recounts these events. "A virgin has given birth," says the midwife, "and you know that's impossible." This mystery is not comprehensible to the common person who has not been initiated. So Salome visits the cave, declaring that she cannot believe the midwife's claim unless she is able to insert her finger into Mary's vagina and examine it. Presumably she is searching for evidence of an unbroken hymen, but since Mary will have already had her hymen broken in childbirth the gesture seems more symbolic than literal. With this, Mary is subjected to yet another test of her virginity. The midwife instructs Mary to position herself for this examination, and Mary complies. When Salome inserts her finger, however, the woman's entire hand is consumed by flames because of her unceremonious transgression of Mary's body as well as her disbelief. Recall that Mary has worked with the fire element in her first chakra, so no wonder Salome gets burned!

The doubting woman gets down on her knees and begs God for mercy on the grounds that she has been healing people in his name.

When a heavenly messenger appears instructing her to pick up the newborn, Salome complies, and her hand is restored, which demonstrates that Jesus's advanced healing abilities are present from day one. The messenger instructs her not to report the marvels she has seen until the child gets to Jerusalem.

We can see that the story of the two midwives echoes Mary's vision about the two different ways people will use the mission of Jesus: one for liberation and personal growth, and the other for control and suffering. One midwife views the events with an open-mindedness to the fifth dimension in which miracles are possible. The other is confined to three-dimensional reality, to the point that she engages in the humiliating violation of the womb of the Sacred Feminine due to her doubt. Clearly, the gospel is conveying a lesson about discernment and spiritual openness, something worth pondering.

FOR WHOM ARE THE HOLY MEN'S GIFTS?

The gospel next relates how Joseph's caravan, now including Baby Jesus, prepares to set off for home, but another event intervenes. This is the arrival of the *magoi,* the three holy men who have come to the region seeking "the newborn King of the Judeans."* Along their route they have told people that they made this journey because they saw the newborn's star from their home in the East and wish to pay homage to him.

It turns out that Herod, the Jewish leader of Judea under Rome, has heard the claim of the holy men and is deeply threatened by the possibility of insurgence that this could foment, so he sends his agents to bring the holy men in for questioning. He asks them what has been written about this *Christos,* this "Annointed One," and where he has supposedly been born. They tell him that the scriptures indicate that the birth has taken place in Bethlehem of Judea.†

Herod asks them what sign they have seen regarding the one who has

---

*This passage is similar to Matthew 2, but with some interesting elaborations, such as the quality of the star in the sky that these men have been following.

†Presumably this is a reference to Micah 5:2, where such a ruler is prophesied.

been born a king. They reply that they saw a star of such brilliance that it dimmed the other stars in the sky, and they knew that this sign heralded a king for Israel. Herod deceptively instructs them to continue their search and to report back to him when they have located the child so that he, too, can pay homage to him. Clearly, however, homage is the last thing on his mind. The holy men depart, once again following the star they had witnessed in the East. They continue walking until the star is directly overhead, and there they find the cave with Mary and Jesus in it. They take out from their pouches their gifts to honor this divinely born king: gold, frankincense, and myrrh. After paying their respects, they receive information from a divine messenger to return to their own country by a route that will have them bypass Herod.

These holy men visiting from the East are most likely priests of the Persian (modern-day Iran) faith known as Zoroastrianism, because the Greek term used to describe these men, *magos,* comes from old Persian words that refer to members of a priestly caste of this religion. What's more, the apocryphal text known as the Syriac Infancy Gospel states explicitly in the third chapter that these holy men are pursuing a prophecy from their prophet, Zoradascht (Zoroaster). As part of their religion, these priests paid particular attention to the stars and gained an international reputation for astrology, which was at that time highly regarded as a science.[5] Like the priests of the Hebrew temples, they are oracles and prophets, able to receive divine information directly.

I contend that the star they are following references the astral or interdimensional location of the soul to be born. We see this idea among many indigenous peoples around the world, including Native American cultures that speak of "star beings" as those intelligences that have long assisted humanity with their healing, soul growth, and evolution.* At times, these intelligences have communicated through telepathic means, divinations, astrological configurations, the utterances of oracle priestesses and priests, and more. At other times they have been known to

---

*See, for example, the description of the 35th annual Native American Elders Gathering, held at the Sunray Peace Village in Vermont in July 2019, on the Sunray Meditation Society and Sunray Peace Village website.

incarnate in human form, as was the case with the historical leader known as the Peacemaker, of the Iroquois Confederacy. The origins of these star allies have been listed variously as Sirius, the Pleiades, and other star systems. Clearly, however, what is being described by the magoi may be not a precise astronomical origin place for this new spiritual king, but rather a domain more generally found in other-dimensional reality.

As to the gifts of these magoi, gold is typically a symbol of royalty and also a form of currency; frankincense, which is an incense, has been a symbol of holiness and connection with the Divine because it was burned in temples; and myrrh, an embalming oil, is a symbol of death. Mary will become the most hallowed leader among Jesus's followers and will claim the authority of Hebrew priests for herself by burning incense in holy places. She will also work with Jesus's body and soul in profound ways at the time of his death by crucifixion, in a way that may have involved the anointing of his body. No doubt gold is a currency that she and her family at times relied on to finance their divine ministry. I propose, then, that these gifts of the magoi are not for Jesus, but for Mary herself, and that they are a sign that these wise holy men are honoring her for her own profound gift to humanity.

HUNTING DOWN THE HOLY FAMILY

In the Birth of Mary we next learn that when Herod discovers that the holy men have evaded him, he is enraged. He sends out executioners to kill all the infants two years old and younger as a means of rooting out and eradicating the prophesied king. The text expands on what is presented in Matthew 2, offering a dramatic story involving Mary, Elizabeth, and Zechariah.

When Mary hears about Herod's activities, she takes her child, wraps him in strips of cloth, and hides him in a feeding trough used by cattle.* Meanwhile, Elizabeth, who by now has given birth to John,

---

*Note that these details differ from Luke 2:7, where the wrapping happens immediately after Jesus's birth, and Matthew 2:13–15, where Mary and Joseph flee with Jesus to Egypt.

takes her baby up into the hill country. Frightened, weary, and finding no place to hide him, she cries out loud to the "divine mountain" to take them both in. Given that they are under the protection of a divine messenger, the mountain splits open, revealing light within, and envelopes both mother and child. Many traditions around the world consider mountains to be feminine in nature, a form of the Mother Goddess. So here again, as with the cave, the gospel acknowledges the power of the sacred feminine to harbor, heal, and protect her people.

Clearly Jesus is not the only one specifically being hunted down, because the text next tells us that Herod has also keyed into the infant John. His agents break in on Zechariah while he is serving at the altar as high priest and command him to tell them where he has hidden the boy. Zechariah, no longer mute, resists, giving the excuse that since he is busy ministering to God in the temple there is no way he can presently know where John is. When the agents report this back to Herod, the king becomes even angrier and expresses his fear that perhaps it is John who will be the one to rule over Israel. I believe this indicates that Herod has become aware of the divine nature of John's conception and knows that he is an avatar who, as such, will have high-level powers and leadership abilities. John thus poses a real threat to Herod's power and must be dispensed with. Herod sends the agents back to Zechariah to threaten him with death if he doesn't reveal the whereabouts of his son (recall, however, that John is really Elizabeth's divinely conceived child). Zechariah declares that he is ready to be martyred, and Herod's agents murder him at daybreak with no witnesses around. He has taken the hit to protect John the avatar.

Later in the day, the priests of the temple become worried when Zechariah doesn't show up during the customary hour for greetings and blessings. One of them summons his courage, enters the sanctuary, and sees dried blood next to the altar. Although he finds no body, at this location in the temple where it is customary for the high priest to be in communication with divine messengers the priest hears a voice telling him of Zechariah's murder and proclaiming that the high priest's blood should not be cleaned up until his avenger appears. Frightened, the priest goes out to share what he has seen and heard with his fellow priests. The other priests screw up their courage and file into the inner sanctum. When they see what has happened, they are horrified. We hear that the "walls cry out" and the priests "rip their robes from top to bottom." They disclose the situation to the tribes, and the bewildered people go into formal mourning for three days and three nights.

After the prescribed grieving period, the priests deliberate about whom they should appoint to the position of high priest. They cast lots, and a man named Simeon is divinely chosen. The gospel tells us that this is a man divinely ordained to not die until he has laid eyes on the "Annointed One" in the flesh. This indicates to them that the time of the promised avatar has come.

JAMES WRITES IN EXILE, BLESSED BY SOPHIA

Here the gospel concludes. The author provides a coda in which he identifies himself as James and reveals that he has written this account at the time when an uproar arose in Jerusalem at the death of Herod. He states that to escape this dangerous situation he has found refuge in the wilderness, where he was granted the Sophia, the wisdom, to write the words down.

This claim of authorship connects the date of Mary's gospel to the death of Herod in 4 BCE, an event also mentioned in Matthew 2:19 and generally considered the approximate year of Jesus's birth. Such dating would make this James an eyewitness to much that has been written in the gospel, particularly since the time Mary was first taken in by Joseph.

It is important to our conclusion of this great journey that we note that James states he was granted the Sophia, the divinely inspired wisdom, to write down all he has recorded. Although James credits God with granting this Sophia, we can read in his use of the term his affirmation that his writing is infused with the mysteries of the Sacred Feminine. Certainly, from all that we have explored in this book, this is indeed the case. His narrative is no mere report; it is nothing less than a mystical revelation, a revelation that has been more or less concealed until the present, when we have finally reclaimed enough information about the secret practice of divine birth to properly interpret what James is talking about.

We also receive in James's closing words our final clue as to why he has had to reveal and conceal the mysteries presented therein: He lives in a violent world in which the Holy Family and anyone associated with them are in danger of persecution, torture, and death. Writing such a document to preserve for humanity what he can about the early life of the Blessed Mother has been an act of great courage.

This concludes the epic story of Anne, Joachim, Mary, the infant Jesus, Joseph, Elizabeth, the infant John the Baptist, and Zechariah, as conveyed in Mary's cast-off gospel.

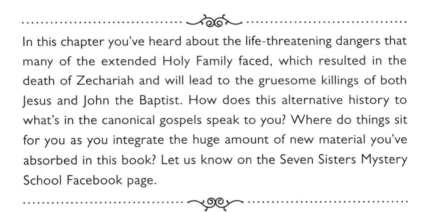

In this chapter you've heard about the life-threatening dangers that many of the extended Holy Family faced, which resulted in the death of Zechariah and will lead to the gruesome killings of both Jesus and John the Baptist. How does this alternative history to what's in the canonical gospels speak to you? Where do things sit for you as you integrate the huge amount of new material you've absorbed in this book? Let us know on the Seven Sisters Mystery School Facebook page.

EPILOGUE

Going Forward with the Newly Revealed Mary

We have been on quite a journey together, a journey to understand Mary through the written word that has never before been undertaken in quite this way. We have opened a whole new door to understanding Mary as a high priestess, a great adept, a living embodiment of the Great Goddess. We have come to understand her not as a pawn of larger forces whose obedience should serve as a model for the rest of us. We can now see her not as a virgin who lacked sexuality and whose "moral purity" should serve as a repressive model for women. Rather, we can appreciate her as an active holy woman who redirected her eros into drawing onto the earth plane another great being who would greatly assist humanity.

All that we have considered can help us make sense, at long last, of the story of Mary's divine conception of Jesus. With this exploration we are no longer left having to reject this story as a fiction that flies in the face of reality. We have been shown the reasons for, and some of the mechanisms of, the practice of divine birth as a pursuit of certain spiritually elevated women, and this practice lies at the foundation of Judaism, Christianity, Islam, and other world religions. We have been shown how and why such women would have chosen this path as a means of world service, including Mary herself; her ancestor Sarah; her mother, Anne; and her (possible) aunt, Elizabeth.

As revelatory as this study has been, it nevertheless still has gaps that leave unanswered some burning questions. What else did Mary need to know and do in order to conceive Jesus, aside from the hints her gospel dangles in front of us? What were the full teachings she received from her mother, from Elizabeth, from her elder sister priestesses, from the heavenly messengers? What were her prayers and practices?

And then, what was her life like while Jesus was alive and after his crucifixion? How did she relate to her son, to the Magdalene, to the priests and priestesses of the early church?

What of her death, as well? How did she ascend to full goddesshood, as the history of divine birth we have been exploring suggests she would have accomplished?

Our questions are personal, as well. What does embracing Mary as an active agent in divine birth mean for us today, especially for spiritually oriented women who wish to teach, preach, and conceive children, whether actual offspring or our creative projects and actions in the world? How can we know what she knows and make the leap from her to us?

There are many questions, many answers, and many possibilities.

May you ponder in your heart all that has been revealed here. May you continue to receive your own revelations that allow you to connect with Mary in her full power. May this strengthen you in your own life and in your work to assist the world in this hugely transitional time.

Birth of Mary
(Infancy Gospel of James)

The following translation of the Birth of Mary (Infancy Gospel of James) is from *The Infancy Gospel of James and Thomas* by Ronald Hock, used by permission.

CHAPTER 1

(1) According to the records of the twelve tribes of Israel, there once was a very rich man named Joachim. (2) He always doubled the gifts he offered to the Lord, (3) and would say to himself, "One gift, representing my prosperity, will be for all the people; the other, offered for forgiveness, will be my sin-offering to the Lord God." (4) Now the great day of the Lord was approaching, and the people of Israel were offering their gifts. (5) And Reubel confronted Joachim and said, "You're not allowed to offer your gifts first because you haven't produced an Israelite child." (6) And Joachim became very upset and went to the book of the twelve tribes of the people, saying to himself, "I'm going to check the book of the twelve tribes of Israel to see whether I'm the only one in Israel who hasn't produced a child." (7) And

he searched (the records) and found that all the righteous people in Israel did indeed have children. (8) And he remembered the patriarch Abraham because in his last days the Lord God had given him a son, Isaac. (9) And so he continued to be very upset and did not see his wife but banished himself to the wilderness and pitched his tent there. (10) And Joachim fasted "forty days and forty nights." (11) He would say to himself, "I will not go back for food or drink until the Lord my God visits me. Prayer will be my food and drink."

CHAPTER 2

(1) Now his wife Anna was mourning and lamenting on two counts: "I lament my widowhood and I lament my childlessness." (2) The great day of the Lord approached, however, (3) and Juthine her slave said to her, "How long are you going to humble yourself? Look, the great day of the Lord has arrived, and you're not supposed to mourn. (4) Rather, take this headband which the mistress of the workshop gave to me, but which I'm not allowed to wear because I'm your slave and because it bears a royal insignia." (5) And Anna said, "Get away from me! I won't take it. The Lord God has greatly shamed me. Maybe a trickster has given you this, and you've come to make me share in your sin." (6) And Juthine the slave replied, "Should I curse you just because you haven't paid any attention to me? The Lord God has made your womb sterile so you won't bear any children for Israel." (7) Anna, too, became very upset. She took off her mourning clothes, washed her face, and put on her wedding dress. (8) Then, in the middle of the afternoon, she went down to her garden to take a walk. She spied a laurel tree and sat down

under it. **(9)** After resting, she prayed to the Lord: "O God of my ancestors, bless me and hear my prayer, just as you blessed our mother Sarah and gave her a son, Isaac."

CHAPTER 3

(1) And Anna looked up toward the sky and saw a nest of sparrows in the laurel tree. **(2)** And immediately Anna began to lament, saying to herself: "Poor me! Who gave birth to me? What sort of womb bore me? **(3)** For I was born under a curse in the eyes of the people of Israel. And I've been reviled and mocked and banished from the temple of the Lord my God. **(4)** Poor me! What am I like? I am not like the birds of the sky, because even the birds of the sky reproduce in your presence, O Lord. **(5)** Poor me! What am I like? I am not like the domestic animals, because even the domestic animals bear young in your presence, O Lord. **(6)** Poor me! What am I like? I am not like the wild animals of the earth, because even the animals of the earth reproduce in your presence, O Lord. **(7)** Poor me! What am I like? I am not like these waters, because even these waters are productive in your presence, O Lord. **(8)** Poor me! What am I like? I am not like this earth, because even the earth produces its crops in season and blesses you, O Lord."

CHAPTER 4

(1) Suddenly a messenger of the Lord appeared to her and said: "Anna, Anna, the Lord God has heard your prayer. You will conceive and give birth, and your child will be talked about all over the world." **(2)** And Anna said, "As the Lord God lives, whether

I give birth to a boy or a girl, I'll offer it as a gift to the Lord my God, and it will serve him its whole life." **(3)** And right then two messengers reported to her: "Look, your husband Joachim is coming with his flocks. **(4)** You see, a messenger of the Lord had come down to Joachim and said, 'Joachim, Joachim, the Lord God has heard your prayer. Get down from there. Look, your wife Anna is pregnant.'" **(5)** And Joachim went down right away and summoned his shepherds with these instructions: "Bring me ten lambs without spot or blemish, and the ten lambs will be for the Lord God. **(6)** Also, bring me twelve tender calves, and the twelve calves will be for the priests and the council of elders. **(7)** Also, one hundred goats, and one hundred goats will be for the whole people. **(8)** And so Joachim came with his flocks, while Anna stood at the gate. **(9)** Then she spotted Joachim approaching with his flocks and rushed out and threw her arms around his neck: "Now I know that the Lord God has blessed me greatly. This widow is no longer a widow, and I, once childless, am now pregnant!" **(10)** And Joachim rested the first day at home.

CHAPTER 5

(1) But on the next day, as he was presenting his gifts, he thought to himself, "If the Lord God has really been merciful to me, the polished disc on the priest's headband will make it clear to me." **(2)** And so Joachim was presenting his gifts and paying attention to the priest's headband until he went up to the altar of the Lord. And he saw no sin in it. **(3)** And Joachim said, "Now I know that the Lord God has been merciful to me and has forgiven me all my sins." **(4)** And he came down from the temple of the Lord acquitted and went back home. **(5)** And so her pregnancy came to term, and in the ninth month Anna gave birth. (6) And she said to the midwife, "Is it a boy or a girl?" (7) And her midwife said, "A girl." (8) And Anna said, "I have been greatly honored this day." Then the midwife put the child to bed. (9) When, however, the prescribed days were completed, Anna cleansed herself of the flow of blood. (10) And she offered her breast to the infant and gave her the name Mary.

CHAPTER 6

(1) Day by day the infant grew stronger. (2) When she was six months old, her mother put her on the ground to see if she could stand. She walked seven steps and went to her mother's arms. (3) Then her mother picked her up and said, "As the Lord my God lives, you will never walk on this ground again until I take you into the temple of the Lord." (4) And so she turned her bedroom into a sanctuary and did not permit anything profane or unclean to pass the child's lips. (5) She sent for the undefiled daughters of the Hebrews, and they kept her amused. (6) Now the child had her first birthday, and Joachim gave a great banquet and invited the high priests, priests, scholars, council of elders, and all the people of Israel. (7) Joachim presented the child to the priests, and they blessed her: "God of our fathers, bless this child and give her a name which will be on the lips of future generations forever." (8) And everyone said, "So be it. Amen." (9) He presented her to the high priests, and they blessed her: "Most high God, look on this child and bless her with the ultimate blessing, one which cannot be surpassed." (10) Her mother then took her up to the sanctuary—the bedroom—and gave her breast to the child. (11) And Anna composed a song for the Lord

God: "I will sing a sacred song to the Lord my God because he has visited me and taken away the disgrace attributed to me by my enemies. (12) The Lord my God has given me the fruit of his righteousness, single yet manifold before him. (13) Who will announce to the sons of Reubel that Anna has a child at her breast? 'Listen, listen, you twelve tribes of Israel: Anna has a child at her breast!'" (14) Anna made her rest in the bedroom—the sanctuary—and then went out and began serving her guests. (15) When the banquet was over, they left in good spirits and praised the God of Israel.

CHAPTER 7

(1) Many months passed, but when the child reached two years of age, Joachim said, "Let's take her up to the temple of the Lord, so that we can keep the promise we made, or else the Lord will be angry with us and our gift will be unacceptable." (2) And Anna said, "Let's wait until she is three, so she won't miss her father or mother." (3) And Joachim agreed: "Let's wait." (4) When the child turned three years of age, Joachim said, "Let's send for the undefiled Hebrew daughters. (5) Let them each take a lamp and light it, so the child won't turn back and have her heart captivated by things outside the Lord's temple." (6) And this is what they did until the time they ascended to the Lord's temple. (7) The priest welcomed her, kissed her, and blessed her: "The Lord God has exalted your name among all generations. (8) In you the Lord will disclose his redemption to the people of Israel during the last days." (9) And he sat her down on the third step of the altar, and the Lord showered favor on her. (10) And she danced, and the whole house of Israel loved her.

CHAPTER 8

(1) Her parents left for home marveling and praising and glorifying the Lord God because the child did not look back at them. (2) And Mary lived in the temple of the Lord. She was fed there like a dove, receiving her food from the hand of a heavenly messenger. (3) When she turned twelve, however, there was a meeting of the priests. "Look," they said, "Mary has turned twelve in the temple of the Lord. (4) What should we do with her so she won't pollute the sanctuary of the Lord our God?" (5) And they said to the high priest, "You stand at the altar of the Lord. Enter and pray about her, and we'll do whatever the Lord God discloses to you." (6) And so the high priest took the vestment with the twelve bells, entered the Holy of Holies, and began to pray about her. (7) And suddenly a messenger of the Lord appeared: "Zechariah, Zechariah, go out and assemble the widowers of the people and have them each bring a staff. (8) She will become the wife of the one to whom the Lord God shows a sign." (9) And so heralds covered the surrounding territory of Judea. The trumpet of the Lord sounded and all the widowers came running.

CHAPTER 9

(1) And Joseph, too, threw down his carpenter's axe and left for the meeting. (2) When they had all gathered, they went to the high priest with their staffs. (3) After the high priest had collected everyone's staff, he entered the temple and began to pray. (4) When he had finished his prayer, he took the staffs and went out and began to give them back to each man. (5) But there was

no sign on any of them. Joseph got the last staff. (6) Suddenly a dove came out of this staff and perched on Joseph's head. (7) "Joseph, Joseph," the high priest said, "you've been chosen by lot to take the virgin of the Lord into your care and protection." (8) But Joseph objected: "I already have sons and I'm an old man; she's only a young woman. I'm afraid that I'll become the butt of jokes among the people of Israel." (9) And the high priest responded, "Joseph, fear the Lord your God and remember what God did to Dathan, Abiron, and Kore*: the earth was split open and they were all swallowed up because of their objection. (10) So now, Joseph, you ought to take heed so that the same thing won't happen to your family." (11) And so out of fear Joseph took her into his care and protection. (12) He said to her, "Mary, I've gotten you from the temple of the Lord, but now I'm leaving you at home. I'm going away to build houses, but I'll come back to you. The Lord will protect you."

CHAPTER 10

(1) Meanwhile, there was a council of the priests, who agreed: "Let's make a veil for the temple of the Lord." (2) And the high priest said, "Summon the true virgins from the tribe of David." (3) And so the temple assistants left and searched everywhere and found seven. (4) And the high priest then remembered the girl Mary, that she, too, was from the tribe of David and was pure in God's eyes. (5) And so the temple assistants went out and got her. (6) And they took the maidens into the temple of the Lord. (7) And the high priest said, "Cast lots for me to

---

*More commonly spelled as Korah.

decide who'll spin which threads for the veil: the gold, the white, the linen, the silk, the violet, the scarlet, and the true purple." (8) And the true purple and scarlet threads fell to Mary. And she took them and returned home. (9) Now it was at this time that Zechariah became mute, and Samuel took his place until Zechariah regained his speech. (10) Meanwhile, Mary had taken up the scarlet thread and was spinning it.

CHAPTER 11

(1) And she took her water jar and went out to fill it with water. (2) Suddenly there was a voice saying to her, "Greetings, favored one! The Lord is with you. Blessed are you among women." (3) Mary began looking around, both right and left, to see where the voice was coming from. (4) She became terrified and went home. After putting the water jar down and taking up the purple thread, she sat down on her chair and began to spin. (5) A heavenly messenger suddenly stood before her: "Don't be afraid, Mary. You see, you've found favor in the sight of the Lord of all. You will conceive by means of his word." (6) But as she listened, Mary was doubtful and said, "If I actually conceive by the Lord, the living God, will I also give birth the way women usually do?" (7) And the messenger of the Lord replied, "No, Mary, because the power of God will overshadow you. Therefore, the child to be born will be called holy, son of the Most High. (8) And you will name him Jesus—the name means 'he will save his people from their sins.'" (9) And Mary said, "Here I am, the Lord's slave before him. I pray that all you've told me comes true."

CHAPTER 12

(1) And she finished (spinning) the purple and the scarlet thread and took her work up to the high priest. (2) The high priest accepted them and praised her and said, "Mary, the Lord God has extolled your name and so you will be blessed by all the generations of the earth." (3) Mary rejoiced and left to visit her relative Elizabeth. (4) She knocked at the door. Elizabeth heard her, tossed aside the scarlet thread, ran to the door, and opened it for her. (5) And she blessed her and said, "Who am I that the mother of my Lord should visit me? You see, the baby inside me has jumped for joy and blessed you." (6) But Mary forgot the mysteries which the heavenly messenger Gabriel had spoken, and she looked up to the sky and said, "Who am I, Lord, that every generation on earth will congratulate me?" (7) She spent three months with Elizabeth. (8) Day by day her womb kept swelling. And so Mary became frightened, returned home, and hid from the people of Israel. (9) She was just sixteen years old when these mysterious things happened to her.

CHAPTER 13

(1) She was in her sixth month when one day Joseph came home from his building projects, entered his house, and found her pregnant. (2) He struck himself in the face, threw himself to the ground on sackcloth, and began to cry bitterly: "What sort of face should I present to the Lord God? (3) What prayer can I say on her behalf since I received her as a virgin from the temple of the Lord God and didn't protect her? (4) Who has set this

trap for me? Who has done this evil deed in my house? Who has lured this virgin away from me and violated her? (5) The story of Adam has been repeated in my case, hasn't it? For just as Adam was praying when the serpent came and found Eve alone, deceived her, and corrupted her, so the same thing has happened to me." (6) So Joseph got up from the sackcloth and summoned Mary and said to her, "God has taken a special interest in you—how could you have done this? (7) Have you forgotten the Lord your God? Why have you brought shame on yourself, you who were raised in the Holy of Holies and fed by a heavenly messenger?" (8) But she began to cry bitter tears: "I'm innocent. I haven't had sex with any man." (9) And Joseph said to her, "Then where did the child you're carrying come from?" (10) And she replied, "As the Lord my God lives, I don't know where it came from."

CHAPTER 14

(1) And Joseph became very frightened and no longer spoke with her as he pondered what he was going to do with her. (2) And Joseph said to himself, "If I try to cover up her sin, I'll end up going against the law of the Lord. (3) And if I disclose her condition to the people of Israel, I'm afraid that the child inside her might be heaven-sent and I'll end up handing innocent blood over to a death sentence. (4) So what should I do with her? (I know,) I'll divorce her quietly." (5) But when night came a messenger of the Lord suddenly appeared to him in a dream and said: "Don't be afraid of this girl, because the child in her is the holy spirit's doing. (6) She will have a son and you will name him Jesus—the name means 'he will save his people from their

sins.'" **(7)** And Joseph got up from his sleep and praised the God of Israel, who had given him this favor. **(8)** And so he began to protect the girl.

CHAPTER 15

(1) Then Annas the scholar came to him and said to him, "Joseph, why haven't you attended our assembly?" **(2)** And he replied to him, "Because I was worn out from the trip and rested my first day home." **(3)** Then Annas turned and saw that Mary was pregnant. **(4)** He left in a hurry for the high priest and said to him, "You remember Joseph, don't you—the man you yourself vouched for? Well, he has committed a serious offense." **(5)** And the high priest asked, "In what way?" **(6)** "Joseph has violated the virgin he received from the temple of the Lord," he replied. "He had his way with her and hasn't disclosed his action to the people of Israel." **(7)** And the high priest asked him, "Has Joseph really done this?" **(8)** And he replied, "Send temple assistants and you'll find the virgin pregnant." **(9)** And so the temple assistants went and found her just as Annas had reported, and then they brought her, along with Joseph, to the court. **(10)** "Mary, why have you done this?" the high priest asked her. "Why have you humiliated yourself? **(11)** Have you forgotten the Lord your God, you who were raised in the Holy of the Holies and were fed by heavenly messengers? **(12)** You of all people, who heard their hymns and danced for them—why have you done this?" **(13)** And she wept bitterly: "As the Lord God lives, I stand innocent before him. Believe me, I have not had sex with any man." **(14)** And the high priest said, "Joseph, why have you done this?" **(15)** And Joseph said, "As the Lord lives, I am innocent where she is concerned."

(16) And the high priest said, "Don't perjure yourself, but tell the truth. You've had your way with her and haven't disclosed this action to the people of Israel. (17) And you haven't humbled yourself under God's mighty hand, so that your offspring might be blessed." (18) But Joseph was silent.

CHAPTER 16

(1) Then the high priest said, "Return the virgin you received from the temple of the Lord." (2) And Joseph, bursting into tears. . . . (3) And the high priest said, "I'm going to give you the Lord's drink test, and it will disclose your sin clearly to both of you." (4) And the high priest took the water and made Joseph drink it and sent him into the wilderness, but he returned unharmed. (5) And he made the girl drink it, too, and sent her into the wilderness. She also came back unharmed. (6) And everybody was surprised because their sin had not been revealed. (7) And so the high priest said, "If the Lord God has not exposed your sin, then neither do I condemn you." And he dismissed them. (8) Joseph took Mary and returned home celebrating and praising the God of Israel.

CHAPTER 17

(1) Now an order came from the Emperor Augustus that everybody in Bethlehem of Judea be enrolled in the census. (2) And Joseph wondered, "I'll enroll my sons, but what am I going to do with this girl? How will I enroll her? (3) As my wife? I'm ashamed to do that. As my daughter? The people of Israel know she's not my daughter. (4) How this is to be decided depends on

the Lord." (5) And so he saddled his donkey and had her get on it. His son led it and Samuel brought up the rear. (6) As they neared the three-mile marker, Joseph turned around and saw that she was sulking. (7) And he said to himself, "Perhaps the baby she is carrying is causing her discomfort." (8) Joseph turned around again and saw her laughing and said to her, "Mary, what's going on with you? One minute I see you laughing and the next minute you're sulking." (9) And she replied, "Joseph, it's because I imagine two peoples in front of me, one weeping and mourning and the other celebrating and jumping for joy." (10) Halfway through the trip Mary said to him, "Joseph, help me down from the donkey—the child inside me is about to be born." (11) And he helped her down and said to her, "Where will I take you to give you some privacy, since this place is out in the open?"

CHAPTER 18

(1) He found a cave nearby and took her inside. He stationed his sons to guard her (2) and went to look for a Hebrew midwife in the country around Bethlehem. (3) "Now I, Joseph, was walking along and yet not going anywhere. (4) I looked up at the vault of the sky and saw it standing still, and then at the clouds and saw them paused in amazement, and at the birds of the sky suspended in midair. (5) As I looked on the earth, I saw a bowl lying there and workers reclining around it with their hands in the bowl; (6) some were chewing and yet did not chew; some were picking up something to eat and yet did not pick it up; and some were putting food in their mouths and yet did not do so. (7) Instead, they were all looking upward. (8) I saw sheep being driven along and yet the sheep stood still; (9) the shepherd

was lifting his hand to strike them, and yet his hand remained raised. (10) And I observed the current of the river and saw goats with their mouths in the water and yet they were not drinking. (11) Then all of a sudden everything and everybody went on with what they had been doing."

CHAPTER 19

(1) "Then I saw a woman coming down from the hill country, and she asked, 'Where are you going, sir?' (2) I replied, 'I am looking for a Hebrew midwife.' (3) She inquired, 'Are you an Israelite?' (4) I told her, 'Yes.' (5) And she said, 'And who's the one having a baby in the cave?' (6) I replied, 'My fiancée.' (7) And she continued, 'She isn't your wife?' (8) I said to her, 'She is Mary, who was raised in the temple of the Lord; I obtained her by lot as my wife. (9) But she's not really my wife; she's pregnant by the holy spirit.' (10) The midwife said, 'Really?'" (11) Joseph responded, "Come and see." (12) And the midwife went with him. (13) As they stood in front of the cave, a dark cloud overshadowed it. (14) The midwife said, "I've really been privileged, because today my eyes have seen a miracle in that salvation has come to Israel." (15) Suddenly the cloud withdrew from the cave and an intense light appeared inside the cave, so that their eyes could not bear to look. (16) And a little later that light receded until an infant became visible; he took the breast of his mother Mary. (17) Then the midwife shouted: "What a great day this is for me because I've seen this new miracle!" (18) And the midwife left the cave and met Salome and said to her, "Salome, Salome, let me tell you about a new marvel: a virgin has given birth, and you know that's impossible!" (19) And Salome replied, "As the

Lord my God lives, unless I insert my finger and examine her, I will never believe that a virgin has given birth."

CHAPTER 20

(1) The midwife entered and said, "Mary, position yourself for an examination. You are facing a serious test." (2) And so Mary, when she heard these instructions, positioned herself, and Salome inserted her finger into Mary. (3) And then Salome cried aloud and said, "I'll be damned because of my transgression and my disbelief; I have put the living God on trial. (4) Look! My hand is disappearing! It's being consumed by flames!" (5) Then Salome fell on her knees in the presence of the Lord, with these words: "God of my ancestors, remember me because I am a descendant of Abraham, Isaac, and Jacob. (6) Do not make an example of me for the people of Israel, but give me a place among the poor again. (7) You yourself know, Lord, that I've been healing people in your name and have been receiving my payment from you." (8) And suddenly a messenger of the Lord appeared, saying to her, "Salome, Salome, the Lord of all has heard your prayer. (9) Hold out your hand to the child and pick him up, and then you'll have salvation and joy." (10) Salome approached the child and picked him up with these words: "I'll worship him because he's been born to be king of Israel." (11) And Salome was instantly healed and left the cave vindicated. (12) Then a voice said abruptly, "Salome, Salome, don't report the marvels you've seen until the child goes to Jerusalem."

CHAPTER 21

(1) Joseph was about ready to depart for Judea, but a great uproar was about to take place in Bethlehem in Judea. (2) It all started when astrologers came inquiring, "Where is the newborn king of the Judeans? We're here because we saw his star in the East and have come to pay him homage." (3) When Herod heard about their visit, he was terrified and sent agents to the astrologers. (4) He also sent for the high priests and questioned them in his palace: "What has been written about the Anointed? Where is he supposed to be born?" (5) They said to him, "In Bethlehem, Judea, that's what the scriptures say." (6) And he dismissed them. (7) Then he questioned the astrologers: "What sign have you seen regarding the one who has been born king?" (8) And the astrologers said, "We saw a star of exceptional brilliance in the sky; and it so dimmed the other stars that they disappeared. Consequently, we know that a king was born for Israel. And we have come to pay him homage." (9) Herod instructed them: "Go and begin your search, and if you find him, report back to me, so I can also go and pay him homage." (10) The astrologers departed. And there it was: the star they had seen in the East led them on until they came to the cave; then the star stopped directly above the head of the child. (11) After the astrologers saw him with his mother Mary, they took gifts out of their pouches— gold, pure incense, and myrrh. (12) Since they had been advised by the heavenly messenger not to go into Judea, they returned to their country by another route.

ᴡ

CHAPTER 22

. . . .

(1) When Herod realized he had been duped by the astrologers, he flew into a rage (2) and dispatched his executioners with instructions to kill all the infants two years old and younger. (3) When Mary heard that the infants were being killed, she was frightened (4) and took her child, wrapped him in strips of cloth, and put him in a feeding trough used by cattle. (5) As for Elizabeth, when she heard that they were looking for John, she took him and went up into the hill country. (6) She kept searching for a place to hide him, but there was none to be had. (7) Then she groaned and said out loud, "Mountain of God, please take in a mother with her child." You see, Elizabeth was unable to keep on climbing because her nerve failed her. (8) But suddenly the mountain was split open and let them in. This mountain allowed the light to shine through to her, (9) since a messenger of the Lord was with them for protection.

ᴡ

CHAPTER 23

. . . .

(1) Herod, though, kept looking for John (2) and sent his agents to Zechariah serving at the altar with this message for him: "Where have you hidden your son?" (3) But he answered them, "I am a minister of God, attending to his temple. How should I know where my son is?" (4) So the agents left and reported all this to Herod, who became angry and said, "Is his son going to rule over Israel?" (5) And he sent his agents back with this message for him: "Tell me the truth. Where is your son? Don't you know that I have your life in my power?" (6) And the agents

went and reported this message to him. (7) Zechariah answered, "I am a martyr for God. Take my life. (8) The Lord, though, will receive my spirit because you are shedding innocent blood at the entrance to the temple of the Lord." (9) And so at daybreak Zechariah was murdered, but the people of Israel did not know that he had been murdered.

✲

CHAPTER 24

(1) At the hour of formal greetings the priests departed, but Zechariah did not meet and bless them as was customary. (2) And so the priests waited around for Zechariah, to greet him with prayer and to praise the Most High God. (3) But when he did not show up, they all became fearful. (4) One of them, however, summoned up his courage, entered the sanctuary, and saw dried blood next to the Lord's altar. (5) And a voice said, "Zechariah has been murdered! His blood will not be cleaned up until his avenger appears." (6) When he heard this utterance he was afraid and went out and reported to the priests what he had seen and heard. (7) And they summoned up their courage, entered, and saw what had happened. (8) The panels of the temple cried out, and the priests ripped their robes from top to bottom. (9) They didn't find a corpse, but they did find his blood, now turned to stone. (10) They were afraid and went out and reported to the people that Zechariah had been murdered. (11) When all the tribes of the people heard this, they began to mourn; and they beat their breasts for three days and three nights. (12) After three days, however, the priests deliberated about whom they should appoint to the position of Zechariah. (13) The lot fell to

Simeon. (14) This man, you see, is the one who was informed by the holy spirit that he would not see death until he laid eyes on the Anointed in the flesh.

CHAPTER 25

(1) Now I, James, am the one who wrote this account at the time when an uproar arose in Jerusalem at the death of Herod. (2) I took myself off to the wilderness until the uproar in Jerusalem died down. (3) There I praised the Lord God, who gave me the wisdom to write this account. (4) Grace will be with all those who fear the Lord. Amen. Birth of Mary. Revelation of James. Peace to the writer and the reader.

Additional Teachings
and Resources
from the Author

To be kept abreast of my continuing work on the Blessed Mother and to access the online meditations and courses I offer on Mary, please visit my online school, Seven Sisters Mystery School, at
sevensistersmysteryschool.com
and feel free to sign up for our e-newsletter. I also invite you to offer your responses to this book and anything else you would like to share about Mary on the
Seven Sisters Mystery School Facebook page.

Also by Marguerite Rigoglioso, Ph.D.

The Cult of Divine Birth in Ancient Greece
Virgin Mother Goddesses of Antiquity

Notes

Ancient Greek and Roman references are cited by just author, title, and section, following the common way of citing such works in scholarly literature. These texts can easily be looked up in various print and online sources.

Chapter 2. Revealing the Hidden Mystery
of Divine Birth

1. Plutarch, *Numa* 4.4; see also Plutarch, *Table-Talk* 8.1/718A–B.
2. Rigoglioso, "Bearing the Holy Ones," chapter 3; and Rikala, "Sacred Marriage."
3. "Testament of Reuben" 5:5–6, in Collins, "Sons of Gods," 266.
4. Collins, "Sons of Gods," 259–67, 272, 274.
5. Pindar as quoted in Plato, *Meno* 81b.
6. Suetonius, *De Vita Caesarum—Divus Augustus*, 94.
7. Rigoglioso, *Cult of Divine Birth*, 29–30.
8. Rigoglioso, *Cult of Divine Birth*, 132.
9. Faulkner, "'The Pregnancy of Isis,'" 218–19.
10. Heartsong, *Anna*, 77–78.
11. Poitras, *Parthenogenesis*, 95.
12. Bernard, *Mysteries*, 126, and *Physiological Enigma*, 48–62.
13. See, for example, his lectures "Black Woman as God," "Woman, Man, Child," and "Woman," on YouTube (all three retrieved Jan. 26, 2020).

Chapter 3. Uncovering the Jewel of Mother Mary's
Suppressed Gospel

1. Hock, *Infancy Gospels*, 4.
2. Reames, "Legends of St. Anne, Mother of the Virgin Mary: Introduction," in *Legends*.
3. Hock, *Infancy Gospels*, 27.
4. Kateusz, *Mary*, 6.
5. Kateusz, *Mary*, 5.
6. Bourgeault, *Wisdom Jesus*, 17.
7. Kateusz, *Mary*, 24–48.

Chapter 4. Anne's Divine Conception of Mary

1. Steiner, *Isis,* 52.
2. Teubal, *Sarah,* 110–23.
3. Rigoglioso, *Virgin Mother,* 108–22, 179–81.
4. Hock, *Infancy Gospels,* 35 n2:5.
5. Teubal, *Sarah,* 111–13, 123.
6. Teubal, *Sarah,* 111–13, 123.
7. Rigoglioso, *Virgin Mother,* 109–10.
8. Rigoglioso, *Cult of Divine Birth,* 122–24.
9. Rigoglioso, *Cult of Divine Birth,* 16.
10. Teubal, *Sarah,* 107.
11. Teubal, *Sarah,* 83, 100–102, 119, 123.
12. Teubal, *Sarah,* 88–90.
13. Teubal, *Sarah,* 28–29.
14. Teubal, *Sarah,* 128.
15. Teubal, *Sarah,* 119–21.
16. Teubal, *Sarah,* 120.
17. Teubal, *Sarah,* 119.
18. Heartsong, *Anna,* 94, 103, 126.
19. Philo, *De Cherubim* 12.40 onward.
20. Teubal, *Sarah,* 129–30.
21. Hock, *Infancy Gospels,* 39 n4:4.

Chapter 5. Mary's Childhood Training
for Divine Conception

1. Steiner, *Isis,* 75, 100.
2. Kaleshwar, *Real Life and Teachings,* 29, 61, 141, 278.
3. Hock, *Infancy Gospels,* 43 n6:4.
4. Philo, *De Vita Contemplativa* 3.25.
5. Amazzone, *Goddess Durga,* 69 onward.
6. Worsfold, *History,* 21–23, 53, 59, 60–61.
7. Brooten, *Women Leaders,* throughout, and 6–7 for scholarly arguments on this subject.
8. Reese, *Women,* 7; and Picknett and Prince, *When God Had a Wife.*
9. Kramer, *Sacred Marriage,* 85.
10. Philo, *De Cherubim* 13.43 onward for this discussion.
11. Hock, *Infancy Gospels,* 43 n6:5.
12. Rigoglioso, *Virgin Mother,* 133–34.
13. Rigoglioso, *Cult of Divine Birth,* 46–50, 137.
14. Kaleshwar, *Real Life and Teachings,* 61–64.
15. Philo, *De Vita Contemplative* 3.29.

16. Rigoglioso, *Cult of Divine Birth,* 101–3.
17. Lindner, "Vestal Virgins," 18–20.
18. Lindner, 22; Worsfold, *History,* 48–52.
19. Worsfold, *History,* 16–17.
20. Worsfold, *History,* 23.
21. Worsfold, *History,* 59–60.
22. This reference to "secret rites" intriguingly appears in Stewart and Long's translation of Numa 9:8 in *Plutarch's Lives,* but not in all modern translations of this ancient work.
23. Worsfold, *History,* 26.
24. Worsfold, *History,* 59.
25. Worsfold, *History,* 19, 67.
26. Rigoglioso, *Cult of Divine Birth,* 150.
27. Rigoglioso, *Cult of Divine Birth,* 148, 151.
28. Rigoglioso, *Cult of Divine Birth,* 152.
29. Rigoglioso, *Cult of Divine Birth,* 150.
30. Zervos, "Early Non-Canonical Annunciation," 670–84.
31. Kateusz, *Mary,* 138.

Chapter 6. Mary's Divine Conception of Jesus

1. Rigoglioso, *Cult of Divine Birth,* 54–55, 117–18, 120, 130.
2. Rigoglioso, *Cult of Divine Birth,* 175.
3. Rigoglioso, *Cult of Divine Birth,* 16–17.
4. See Kateusz, *Mary,* 138–39, for this discussion and the accompanying references.
5. Campra, "Gnostic Sophia," 191–207.
6. Steiner, *Isis,* 135.
7. See "The Thunder, Perfect Mind," trans. George W. MacRae, Gnosis.org.
8. Nyberg, "Sacred Prostitution," 309.
9. Nyberg, "Sacred Prostitution," 314 and n31.
10. Hock, *Infancy Gospels,* 53 n12:2.
11. Hock, *Infancy Gospels,* 53 n12:4.
12. Qa'im and Legenhausen, *Jesus,* 62.
13. Hock, *Infancy Gospels,* 55 n12:9.

Chapter 7. Mary's Trials and the Birth of Jesus

1. Aelian, *On Animals* 11.16.
2. Valerius Maximus, 8.1.5; and Augustine, *De Civitate Dei* 10.16.
3. Hock, *Infancy Gospels,* 63 n17:5.
4. Hock, *Infancy Gospels,* 67 n19:16.
5. Boyce, *History,* 10–11; Boyce, *Zoroastrians,* 48; Murray, *Oxford Companion,* 293; and Mitchell, *History,* 387.

Bibliography

Amazzone, Laura. *Goddess Durga and Sacred Female Power*. Lanham, Md.: Hamilton Books, 2010.

Bauckham, Richard. *Jesus and the Eyewitnesses: The Gospels as Eyewitness Testimony*. Grand Rapids, Mich.: Eerdmans, 2006.

Bernard, Raymond. *The Mysteries of Human Reproduction*. Mokelumne Hill, Calif.: Health Research, n.d.

———. *The Physiological Enigma of Woman: The Mystery of Menstruation—Its Cause and Cure*. UK: Reprinted through Lightning Source, n.d.

Bourgeault, Cynthia. *The Wisdom Jesus: Transforming Heart and Mind—A New Perspective on Christ and His Message*. Boulder, Colo.: Shambhala, 2008.

Boyce, Mary. *A History of Zoroastrianism: The Early Period*. Leiden, UK: Brill, 1989.

———. *Zoroastrians: Their Religious Beliefs and Practices*. New York: Routledge, 2001.

Brooten, Bernadette. *Women Leaders in the Ancient Synagogue*. Chico, Calif.: Scholars Press, 1982.

Brown, Francis, C. Briggs, and S. R. Driver. *The Brown–Driver–Briggs Hebrew and English Lexicon*. Peabody, Mass.: Hendrickson Publishers, 1996.

Campra, Angeleen. "The Gnostic Sophia: Divine Generative Virgin." In *Virgin Mother Goddesses of Antiquity*, by Marguerite Rigoglioso, 191–207. New York: Palgrave Macmillan, 2010.

Collins, John J. "The Sons of Gods and the Daughters of Men." In *Sacred Marriages: The Divine-Human Sexual Metaphor from Sumer to Early Christianity*, edited by Martii Nissinen and Risto Uro, 259–74. Winona Lake, Ind.: Eisenbrauns, 2008.

Elder, Linda Bennett. "The Woman Question and Female Ascetics Among the Essenes." *The Biblical Archaeologist* 57, no. 4 (December 1994): 220–34.

Faulkner, Raymond O. "'The Pregnancy of Isis,' a Rejoinder," *The Journal of Egyptian Archaeology* 59 (1973): 218–19.

Gero, Joan M., and Margaret W. Conkey, eds. *Engendering Archaeology: Women and Prehistory*. Oxford; Cambridge, Mass.: B. Blackwell, 1991.

Gimbutas, Marija. *Language of the Goddess*. London: Thames and Hudson, 2001.

Hammer, Jill, and Taya Shere. *The Hebrew Priestess.* Teaneck, N.J.: BenYehuda Press, 2015.

Heartsong, Claire. *Anna, Grandmother of Jesus.* London: Hay House, 2017.

Hock, Ronald F. *The Infancy Gospels of James and Thomas.* Santa Rosa, Calif.: Polebridge Press, 1995.

Kaleshwar, Sri. *The Real Life and Teachings of Jesus Christ.* Penukonda, India: Sri Kaleshwar Publications, 2010.

Kateusz, Ally. *Mary and Early Christian Women: Hidden Leadership.* New York: Palgrave Macmillan, 2019.

Kenyon, Tom, and Judy Sion. *The Arcturian Anthology.* New York: Orb Publishing, 2013.

Kolata, Gina. "Scientist Clones Human Embryos, And Creates an Ethical Challenge." *New York Times,* October 24, 1993.

Kramer, Samuel Noah. *The Sacred Marriage Rite: Aspects of Faith, Myth, and Ritual in Ancient Sumer.* Bloomington, Ind.: Indiana University Press, 1969.

———. *The Sumerians: Their History, Culture and Character.* Chicago: University of Chicago Press, 1963.

Lapinkivi, Pirjo. "The Sumerian Sacred Marriage and Its Aftermath in Later Sources." In *Sacred Marriages: The Divine-Human Sexual Metaphor from Sumer to Early Christianity,* edited by Martii Nissinen and Risto Uro, 7–41. Winona Lake, Ind.: Eisenbrauns, 2008.

Lewis, I. M. *Ecstatic Religion: An Anthropological Study of Spirit Possession and Shamanism.* Middlesex, UK: Penguin, 1971.

Lindner, Molly Morrow McGlannan. "The Vestal Virgins and Their Imperial Patrons." PhD diss., University of Michigan, 1996 (UMI#9624671).

Mitchell, Stephen. *A History of the Later Roman Empire, CE 284–641: The Transformation of the Ancient World.* Hoboken, N.J.: Wiley-Blackwell, 2007.

Murdoch, D. M. *Christ in Egypt: The Horus-Jesus Connection.* Ashland, Oreg.: Stellar House Publishing, 2009.

Murray, Linda. *The Oxford Companion to Christian Art and Architecture.* Oxford: Oxford University Press, 1996.

Nissinen, Martii, and Risto Uro, eds. *Sacred Marriages: The Divine-Human Sexual Metaphor from Sumer to Early Christianity.* Winona Lake, Ind.: Eisenbrauns, 2008.

Nyberg, Kristel. "Sacred Prostitution in the Biblical World?" In *Sacred Marriages: The Divine-Human Sexual Metaphor from Sumer to Early Christianity,* edited by Martii Nissinen and Risto Uro, 305–20. Winona Lake, Ind.: Eisenbrauns, 2008.

Picknett, Lynn, and Clive Prince. *When God Had a Wife: The Fall and Rise of the Sacred Feminine in the Judeo-Christian Tradition.* Rochester, Vt.: Bear and Company, 2019.

Poitras, Den. *Parthenogenesis: Women's Long-Lost Ability to Self-Conceive.* Self-published, 2018.

Qa'im, Mahdi Muntazir, and al-Hajj Muhammad Legenhausen, trans. *Jesus through the Qur'an and Shi'ite Narrations,* Elmhurst, N.Y.: Tahrike Tarsile Qur'an, 2005.

Reames, Sherry L., ed. *Middle English Legends of Women Saints.* Kalamazoo, Mich.: Medieval Institute Publications, 2003.

Reese, Lyn. *Women in the Ancient Near East: Stories and Primary Sources from the Sumerians through the Early Israelites.* Berkeley, Calif.: Women in World History Curriculum, 1999.

Rigoglioso, Marguerite. "Bearing the Holy Ones: A Study of the Cult of Divine Birth in Ancient Greece." PhD diss., California Institute of Integral Studies, 2007 (Dissertation Abstracts International, publ. nr. AAT3286688, DAI-A 68/10).

———. *The Cult of Divine Birth in Ancient Greece.* New York: Palgrave Macmillan, 2009.

———. *Virgin Mother Goddesses of Antiquity.* New York: Palgrave Macmillan, 2010.

Rikala, Mia. "Sacred Marriage in the New Kingdom of Ancient Egypt: Circumstantial Evidence for a Ritual Interpretation." In *Sacred Marriages: The Divine-Human Sexual Metaphor from Sumer to Early Christianity,* edited by Martii Nissinen and Risto Uro, 115–44. Winona Lake, Ind.: Eisenbrauns, 2008.

Steiner, Rudolph. *Isis Mary Sophia.* Great Barrington, Mass.: SteinerBooks 2003.

Stewart, Aubrey, and George Long. *Plutarch's Lives.* Vol. 1. London: George Bell & Sons, 1984. (Accessed on Project Gutenberg)

Subramuniyaswami, Satguru Sivaya. *Dancing with Siva.* Kapaa, Hawaii: Himalayan Academy, 1997.

Teubal, Savina J. *Sarah the Priestess: The First Matriarch of Genesis.* Athens, Ohio: Swallow Press, 1984.

Worsfold, T. Cato. *History of the Vestal Virgins of Rome.* London: Rider and Co., 1934.

Zervos, George. "An Early Non-Canonical Annunciation Story," 670–84, in *Society of Biblical Literature 1997 Seminar Papers.* Evanston, Ill.: American Theological Library Association, 1997.

Index